computer game graphics

Watson-Guptill Publications/New York

liz faber | state

02

First published in the United States in 1998 by Watson-Guptill Publications, a division of BPI Communications, Inc., 1515 Broadway, New York, New York 10036.

Originally published 1998 by Laurence King Publishing
an imprint of Calmann & King Ltd
71 Great Russell Street, London WC1B 3BN

Library of Congress Catalog Card Number: 98-86872

ISBN 0-8230-0883-5

Printed in Italy

design: state (Mark Breslin, Mark Hough, Philip O'Dwyer)

research: Justin Vir

acknowledgments: thanks are due to Michael Hanley for his contribution to the introduction, and also to David Wilson, Doug Johns, Al Carlson, Sam Page, Gordon Mackay, Glen O'Connell, Peter Devery, Mark Hartley, John Bailey, Matt Broughton and Andrea Schneider.

photographic credits: karin slade (52–3); © SI Credit Syndication International/Button (12–13); Hans Staatjes (118–19).

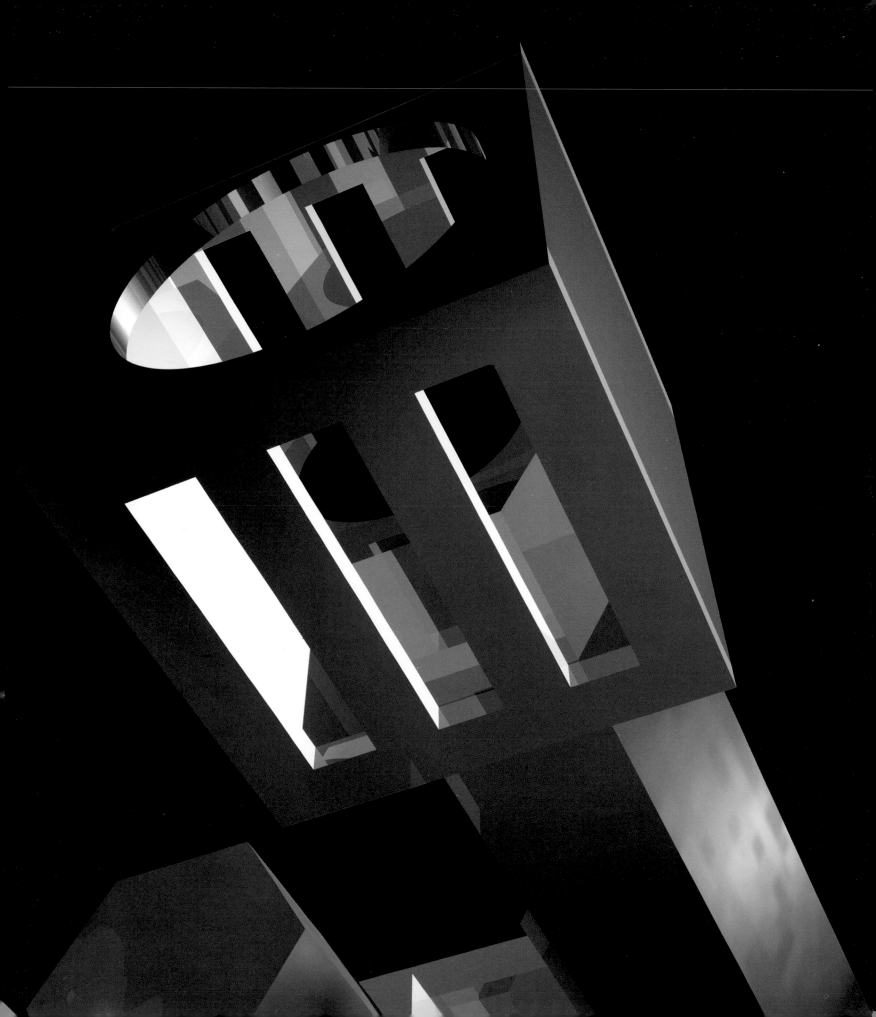

16 kill

38 win

52 drive

68 explore

102 fight

118 control

130 fly

42-43 pong

56 rally x

72 pac-man

74 donkey kong

73 frogger

71 donkey kong jr.

pole position

57

74 mario bros.

channel f

atari vcs
atari 400
atari 600

microvision

intellivision

zx spectrum
colecovision
atari 5200
vectrex

1972

1973

1974

1975

1976

1977

1978

1979

1980

1981

1982

1983

134, 136 f/a 18 hornet
135, 137 f/a 18 korea

133,
138-139,
142-143 f-22 air dominance fighter

122-125 simcity 2000
126-127 command and conquer

128-129 myth

play...ration

106,	way of the exploding fist
108-9	
106	pro-wrestling
106	altered beast
106	wrestlemania
106	wrestlemania steel cage
106	art of fighting
106	street fighter 2 turbo
106	yu yu hakusho
	tokubetsuhen
106	sonic 3
111-115	virtua fighter
110	ultimate mortal kombat
105	tekken 3
116-117	fighter's destiny

75	super mario bros.
76-77	super mario world
82-83	zelda 3
84-85	myst
80	sonic 3
78-79	super mario 64
62-63	super mario kart
64-65	wipeout 2097
58-60	formula 1 '97
61	f1 racing simulation
66-67	gran turismo
88-89	riven
90-93	tomb raider 2
94-97	crash bandicoot 2
98-99	final fantasy vii
100	bladerunner
101	resident evil 2

56	roadfighter
56	rcadblaster
56	buggy boy
56	outrun
56	lcmbard rally
56	fatal run
44-45	tv sports hockey
44-45	horse racing
44-45	super baseball sim
44-45	super tennis
50-51	actua soccer
46-47	winter heat
49	nhl 98

44-45	daley thompson's
	decathlon
44-45	summer games 3
44-45	california games
44-45	konami ping-pong
44-45	bmx airmaster
44-45	power golf
44-45	world court tennis

21	space harrier
21,	r-type
26-27	
21	gradius 2
21	phalanx
21	axelay
21	soldier blade
30	wolfenstein 3d
30	doom
30,	dark forces
30, 31	marathon infinity
32-33	quake
28-29	g-police
34-35	goldeneye
36	mdk
37	turok: dinosaur hunter

nintendo entertainment system

sega master system

atari lynx
turbo grafx 16
nintendo game boy
sega genesis

super nintendo
entertainment system
game gear

sega cd

atari jaguar
3DO interactive multiplayer

sega 32x

sony playstation
sega saturn
nintendo virtual boy

nintendo 64

| 1985 |
| 1986 |
| 1987 |
| 1988 |
| 1989 |
| 1990 |
| 1991 |
| 1992 |
| 1993 |
| 1994 |
| 1995 |
| 1996 |
| 1997 |
| 1998 |

you would have to have been living on Myst Island to have missed the recent explosion in computer games. Worth nothing at its conception in 1969, the global computer games market currently rakes in $17-18 billion a year; the worldwide takings of *Tomb Raider II* outsold the box office takings of *Titanic*. As well as the enormous sums poured into software and hardware platforms, computer games have provided the basis for dozens of spin-off industries, trade magazines, consumer magazines and multimillion-dollar advertising campaigns.

What is it that gives computer games their appeal? Why do we keep coming back again and again to insert another coin, jump that wall, fight off that Nazi guard, shoot those aliens, spin those boxes, run that course, race those cars, jump that gorge, hit that ball or solve that puzzle? The appeal of these games is immense and unstoppable; at the moment we are just beginning to think about the influence that they have on society and its future. Will the computer games explosion affect the way we relate to each other, and our attitude to the world and what it contains, and if so, how?

It is almost forty years since the first computer game was invented by Steve Russell, a student at MIT. *Spacewar* featured two spacecraft that sat on a computer the size of two refrigerators – the first computer to have a screen and not use punch cards (it is interesting to note that as soon as the industry had the raw material to create a computer game, it did). But it was the arrival of *Pong*, in 1972, that indicated a future for these obscure toys created by computer scientists.

Anyone going to the internet and searching for '*Pong* videogame' will find 150,450 discussion groups. *Pong* was the ubiquitous 'blip, blip, blip' electronic game in which players had to 'AVOID MISSING BALL FOR HIGH SCORE'. Atari's version of *Pong* from Christmas 1974 sold 150,000 copies through Sears in the US alone. This was the game that gave birth to the entire games industry.

Like many ephemeral phenomena, *Pong* became a victim of its own success. There were dozens of imitators who pandered to a public that eventually became bored with bouncing a set of electrons across their television sets. Players began to insist on more demanding fare.

They got it with the revolutionary *Space Invaders*, launched in 1978. This was the first game that fully utilized the functionality of the medium on which it sat. Like *Pong*, you could control your manifestation – this time a battle-control cannon shooter set in space. The objective was to destroy the enemy fleet while sliding your craft from side to side, dodging alien missiles. There was no end to *Space Invaders*, and there was always an end to it – final destruction was inevitable: you knew you would die and the excitement was simply when. It was kill or be killed. A simple paradigm from which even today's shooters borrow heavily.

The all-conquering obsession surrounding *Space Invaders* was helped enormously by the launch of the Atari 2600, also in 1978, a cartridge-based computer game machine for which hundreds of titles were developed. Advances after *Space Invaders* came in fits and starts. *Asteroids* was released in 1979; in this game, instead of being rooted to the bottom of the screen, the player's craft was free to fly through space.

Though the game was black and white, its cool vector graphics had great appeal, enabling the player to blast away the oncoming space detritus. In 1980 *Defender* graced our screens. Not only did it have the first split-screen format, it was also the first continually scrolling game.

These games, and a myriad of others like them, such as *Missile Command*, *Tron* and *Zaxxon*, proved to be popular. But they contained no human content. There was nothing to feel fond of or become emotionally attached to – until *Pac-Man* came along in 1980. *Pac-Man* was what the industry had been lacking – a game with personality. Well, five personalities really. Cast in the role of Pac-Man, the player battled against the four ghosts: Pinky, Inky, Clyde and Blinky. In between levels, cute little animations would run as a reward. The many spin-offs included *Mrs Pac-Man*, *Jnr. Pac-Man* and *Pac-Manic*.

Design as a concept in computer games really came into its own with the blossoming into maturity of a fat Italian plumber called Mario, who made his debut in Nintendo's 1982 release *Donkey Kong*. The scheme was for Mario to leap over barrels hurled by an enormous gorilla and climb ladders in order to rescue the ever-elusive Princess Daisy from the gorilla's clutches. Years later, Mario is still leaping through the Mushroom Kingdom in various guises, having been through dozens of versions on several platforms, a move into 3-D and, uniquely, a feature movie starring Bob Hoskins. Mario's legacy can be seen in a myriad of other games, all grouped into the 'platform' genre, such as *Sonic the Hedgehog* (see pages 80–81) and *Crash Bandicoot* (see pages 94–7). There is even talk of Mario diversifying out of platform games and into a role playing game.

How could Nintendo, Mario's creator, have predicted that such an obscure character would capture the game-playing public's imagination, while other equally tenuous characters would not? They couldn't of course, which is why predicting a computer game hit is such a high-stakes business. Chart Track estimate that 30 games a week are published in the UK, but only about five a year are bestsellers. As for the music industry, the big hits subsidize the flops – and there are lots of them. Mario, Pac-Man and Sonic the Hedgehog are the computer game industry's David Bowie, Bruce Springsteen and Michael Jackson.

Console Wars The Atari 5200 dominated as a platform from its release in 1982 until the launch of Nintendo's 8-bit Entertainment System (NES) in 1986; by 1988 this had become North America's best-selling toy. In 1990, *Super Mario Brothers 3* grossed $500 million. In 1991, the NES bequeathed its home entertainment system hegemony to the Super NES, a 16-bit console. Two years previously, however, Sega had launched its 16-bit console, which floundered without a purpose until the birth of the legendary *Sonic the Hedgehog* in 1991. Sonic was Sega's general, leading the charge against Nintendo's Mario and his troops in a head-to-head platform battle for the next four years.

A happy addition to the developing number of computer game genres was the first of a slew of fighting games made possible by 16-bit power. These included *Street Fighter*, the gory *Mortal Kombat*, and *Virtua Fighter*. By this stage it was obvious that technological prowess was key to the success of a computer game console, and that the success of a console was to survive in this most fickle and com-

...etitive of industries. Half a dozen firms had set out to develop the next generation of 32-bit consoles – the first set of machines based on cheap CD-Rom disks rather than chip-heavy cartridges. The machines that came on the market in the mid-1990s are now only dim memories – Commodore's CTV, Philips CD-i and the 3DO. Two 32-bit platforms have, however, managed to survive: the Sega Saturn and the Sony PlayStation.

Wreaking Havoc in Cyberspace While an amount of slaughter was going on in the home console market, four designers in Dallas, Texas were creating some serious bloodshed with the PC format. They were focused on the key to the next generation of powerful gaming technology: networking. In 1993, id Software, a company founded two years earlier by designer John Romero (see pages 32–3) together with three friends (dubbed 'the egos at id' by *Wired* magazine) launched *Doom*. This followed their earlier hit *Wolfenstein 3D*, a violent first-person environmental 'blast 'em off the face of the planet' experience in which the player had to break out of a POW camp and destroy the enemy.

Doom incorporated a marketing master stroke – it was available to download on the internet. What is more, it was networkable – four friends could play it together, and it is much more fun to blow away friends than a computer-generated enemy. Fifteen million copies of shareware *Doom*, the first two levels of the game, were downloaded off the internet. This was enough to whet the appetites of 150,000 PC users who, in 1993, bought the full version of the game, now a fully fledged cult.

The launch of *Doom* and its imitators gave an enormous boost to the console's only contender for power in the computer games universe – the PC. Today, 50 per cent of computer games are run on a PC platform, while the other half play on a dedicated console. Up until 1997, in order to experience arcade-standard graphics and sound in the home, a dedicated games console was required. But now the playing field has changed – advances in the performance of graphics on the PC means the latest generation of these games are a match for Sega and Nintendo's best. This is because of the often quoted Moore's Law.

Moore's Law governs Silicon Valley's most important product cycles for hardware and software alike, games included. In a 1965 speech, chip manufacturer Intel's founder and chair (now emeritus) Gordon Moore made a famous, and famously accurate, observation. He said that with price kept constant, the processing power of microchips doubles every eighteen months. Moore's Law might be the strongest indicator that the final victor in this evolutionary war may very well be the endlessly upgradeable, multi-tasking and increasingly ubiquitous PC. Consumers cannot be expected to purchase a new console each year. This means that developers are faced with platform-based technology restrictions which are only improved every few years. PC developers, however, can fully utilize the latest programming technology, while their customers can upgrade to take advantage of them at their own speed.

On the other hand, because of the infinite combination of PC peripherals and configurations, practically every PC is different. PC game designers have to take their best guess at the ones which will be sitting on their customers' hard drives when their game gets home. To many PC game players' chagrin, this quite frequently doesn't turn out to be the case.

Platform Wars Today, the king of the console market is the Sony PlayStation, which rolled out of the entertainment behemoth's research and development rooms in 1994, blowing away the other 32-bit machines. In the same year Sega released their 32-bit Saturn console. With the Saturn, Sega made a huge mistake: it was too expensive, with not enough games to play. To date, 23 million PlayStations have been sold, compared to 8.2 million Sega Saturns. In 1997, the top PlayStation game title – *Tomb Raider II* – outsold the top Saturn title – *Manx TT* – by a ratio of 10:1, according to *CTW*, the computer entertainment trade weekly. The PlayStation provided a sorely needed shot in the arm for Sony, who was suffering from some poor investment decisions.

Nintendo, with its 16-bit Super NES was left out in the cold by its 32-bit competitors until 1996, when it launched its Nintendo 64. Nintendo expected to obliterate the 32-bit market with its superior brain power. But this is where another golden rule of the games market enters: games maketh the machine. Despite some fantastic titles such as *Goldeneye*, *Diddy Kong Racing* and *Mario 64*, N64 has failed to deliver all it promised – even though the graphics are great. The problem that console manufacturers such as Nintendo face is multiplied enormously because the success of their product relies not only on the quality of their own technology, manufacturing and distribution, but also on that of their key suppliers – the games designers and developers.

A modern computer game takes on average two years, a million pounds and a significant development team to get from the designer's mind to the player's screen. Between this process and the console manufacturers sit the all-powerful publishers – the gods of the industry who decide whether a game idea should get money, and for which platform it should be developed. In the UK, the biggest publisher is Electronic Arts (the largest publisher of home computer software in the world), followed by Nintendo, Sony Microsoft, Virgin, Eidos, Psygnosis, Sega and Ocean. The best game in the world with the wildest graphics and most addictive gameplay will not make a dime without access to the distribution which is in the hands of the publishers. In 1997, 31.8 per cent of all sales in the UK consisted of two titles alone: Eidos's *Tomb Raider* and Electronic Arts' football game, *Fifa*. A mere half a dozen developers have some 70 per cent of the market.

Nevertheless, it is the US market that rules in computer games as much as it does in every other home entertainment or mass media. Americans buy the most and create the most spin-off merchandise. This means that the money they have to offer designers and developers dwarfs that which is available in Europe. The European Leisure Software Publishers Association (ELSPA) claims that the industry is facing an imminent developer drain, as Britain and Europe's best are drawn inexorably across the Atlantic to Silicon Valley and its Hollywood-level salaries.

The situation in the UK for designers and developers, however, is not desperate. According to ELSPA the country's market for computer games grew by 66 per cent in 1997. This growth, combined with a rocketing demand for software technicians in other computing industries (including millennium bug consultants, currently at a well-timed peak), means salaries for people with game-coding skills are also seeing significant growth. However, the industry globally is facing a reduction in the number of programmers...

that it will need, as it develops the technology to create machines that can produce passages, maps and dimensions. The exciting design work of adding features will be left to a smaller number of specialists.

The Format of the Future So we know that good technology is important, and that good games are essential. Does this give us any further insight into the successful game format of the future? Will we play on a dedicated console, or a networked PC? Or a combination of both?

Consoles have the immutable advantage of being specially designed for playing games; that grey box under the television is exclusively for PlayStation games. There is no confusion. The problem that the PC faces as a games platform is that people interact with their PCs in all sorts of ways: doing the accounts, writing letters, surfing the internet or doing the shopping. These are not relaxing tasks, and the upright-sitting-at-a-desk way of interacting with a machine cannot compete with the 'chilling-on-the-sofa' ethos the console enjoys because of its relationship with the television. Moreover, the computer's main method of data input, the keyboard, is over a hundred years old, and is no good at the manually dextrous tasks demanded of so many games.

The holy grail of games platforms, the machine that will win the PC versus console battle, will combine the console's ease of interaction with the breadth of functionality of the PC. The same battle is being waged in the communications industry, as data transmission over networks becomes radically cheaper. Television, telephone, cable and satellite companies are battling over the rights to consumers' viewing time and spending money. Sega is hoping that its new console, Dreamcast, will be the solution. Dreamcast launches in Japan in November 1998, and in the US a year later. The console boasts 128-bit graphics from a reduced instruction set computing central processor. An independent 3-D graphics engine with a dedicated 3-D sound chip, Dreamcast will also be the first console to offer standard networking features for multi-player gaming, bringing together for the first time a console, PC and online gaming. The list of Sega's partners in this venture reads like a *Who's Who* of the electronics industry: Microsoft, Hitachi, NEC, Videologic and Yamaha.

Mirroring the convergence in communications is a convergence between different entertainment media – pop songs appear in movies that were originally computer games, entertainment studios are opening up amusement parks that feature the characters from their films and games, sports celebrities appear in movies (not to mention crowd-drawing court cases on cable TV), and the music industry benefits by providing soundtracks.

Movie characters make great subjects for games because the player is familiar with the plot and the character's identifying features. Successful movie-inspired games include *Batman*, the *Die Hard Trilogy* and *James Bond* – the N64 *Goldeneye* incarnation (the UK's twelfth most profitable game in 1997, and third most profitable N64 game, after two Mario games).

One other modern day entertainment icon, the sports star, is also embroiled in the multi-media mêlée: sport is the gaming genre that borrows most from 'real life'. Sports stars provide great fodder for the char-

acter element that is so important when seeking games players' loyalty. Many successful sports games feature stars such as André Agassi, Jack Nicklaus and Alan Shearer. Sports games have given product placement and billboarding its most successful theatre: punters relate to sports marketing in a game through their familiarity with it via television and real life.

For serious games players, however, plundering ideas and characters from other media or real life is a cop out. 'Authentic' computer games exploit the dimension that gaming provides to a greater extent than any other medium – interactivity. Movie-goers are absolved of all responsibility for their experience once they pay for their ticket and sit down, but if Lara Croft is impaled on stakes at the bottom of a snake pit, the responsibility for this gruesome fate lies entirely with the player. Emotional engagement is much stronger when the main character's life is in your hands.

It is this emotional engagement that makes computer games potentially the most powerful and addictive entertainment medium of all. It is what makes the games such an easy target for politicians and censors who would ban the depiction of violence as they would violence itself. Violence in computer games is a marketing tool; like good graphics, it is a tool that computer game makers have found engages and excites people. John Romero, creator of the disgustingly gory *Doom*, is a target for a lot of censorial abuse. His attitude, however, is that only a very small minority of unstable individuals are affected, and that overall, violent games have the positive effect of providing a release for pent-up tension (see page 33).

Like any other cultural phenomenon, games tend to reflect the values, the design instincts, and the visions and dreams of the societies in which their creators live. American games tend to contain a lot more guns, grit, gore and sex (*Doom*, *Resident Evil*, *Hexen*, *Quake*, *Mortal Kombat* – they don't get gorier). Japanese and European games tend to favour slick graphical depictions of futuristic scenarios (*Wipeout*, *Final Fantasy VII*, *Virtua Fighter*, *G-Police*, *Tekken*). Moreover, Japanese games design splits broadly between heavily manga-influenced beat-em-ups, and a stable of improbably cute cartoon figures, such as Sonic and Mario. While reflecting the cultures in which they are born, computer games also flatten out racial and sexual differences. Where people are depicted, they tend to have racially homogenized features. Michelle Chan, a 'superbabe' who cuts a nice line in denim hot-pants in *Tekken*, epitomizes the racially diverse characters that populate the modern computer game – her mother is a native American, while her father is 'a Hong Kong man'.

Technology is essential in a successful game and so is character, but truly special games are built of three blocks: the third ingredient in the mix is the killer application and the one that many games designers find their greatest challenge and triumph: plot. There is a band of gamers who are fascinated not by speed, adrenalin or manual dexterity challenges, but with the creation of fantasy worlds and the development of intricate universes. Before computer games and games graphics there were interactive role playing games in booklet format, exemplified by the seminal *Dungeons and Dragons*, the quintessential plot-rich booklet, graph and dice-based adventure game. For the first decade of its life, the games industry concentrated on developing products that would have the greatest immediate impact and investment

...etum. This resulted in an abundance of shoot-em-ups and electronic finger and wrist challenges. But Moore's Law, rocketing technological possibilities and the development of graphic techniques have given game producers the ability to experiment with the luxury of gaming plot and storyline.

Myst is the seminal example of plot-led gaming, and the bravest exploration of the gaming medium to date. Set on an island, virtually no characters appear in the game. With no fast action, shooting, sex or violence, *Myst* is as much an exploration of the nature of storytelling, time and history as it is a computer game. *Myst* was developed by brothers Robyn and Rand Miller in 1993, and has been followed up by *Riven*, launched in 1997, a *Myst*-style adventure that once again pushes the boundaries of modern day technological, storytelling and graphical techniques.

What the Miller brothers did with their emotionally jarring, non-violent and deeply intellectual *Myst,* was to bring the concept of the plot firmly back to the centre of the game. *Myst,* however, was not the first computer game to have a depth of plot. In the late 1960s, many of the 'anoraks' who played *Dungeons and Dragons* in their lunchbreaks were actually the people who had access to the first computer technology. The combination of their computer prowess and their gaming interests produced several text-based games where the player would type the direction in which they wished to head, and the computer would reply in text along the lines of: 'A huge fierce green snake bars the way'.

Daikatana, the latest project out of John Romero's ION Storm, includes such elaborate plot devices as a pair of talking characters who act as allies to the human player – a bold departure from standard-issue 3-D carnage. Romero hopes the introduction of deep plot will boost emotional involvement and, eventually, help turn mere games into immersive dramas. In an interview with *Time* magazine in June 1997, he claimed 'the internet is sucking people away from TV like crazy,' and elaborated on his plans to help his game benefit from this convergence of entertainment media: 'every week the latest *Daikatana* episode would be up on our website at say, 9 p.m. It could have new music, new levels, new characters, whatever we could throw over the internet.'

One of the best indications of what an immersive game experience is like is the already legendary *Tomb Raider*. Borrowing from the thrill of exploration found in a platform game, the adrenalin-pumping action of a shoot-em-up, and the strategic and puzzle-solving challenge of a puzzle-based game such as *The Seventh Guest*, *Tomb Raider* captured game players' imaginations in 1996. Cynics may say that the game's success was simply proportional to the size of its protagonist's chest, but *Tomb Raider*'s appeal is more than simply evidence that game players are just teenage boys who are too shy to talk to real girls and instead satisfy themselves by controlling an electronic one. In an article over two pages the *Observer*, (March 1998) asked two thirty-something individuals to explain why they were addicted to following Lara Croft's tomb raiding adventures. The first piece, written by a man, told of how *Tomb Raider* enhanced his relationship with his wife by giving them something to do together – his wife formulated the strategy, while he satisfied himself with the manual agility challenge of bending Lara Croft to her will. The second piece was written from the woman's perspective. She, in fact, says more or less the same thing that *Tomb Raider* presents a mental challenge for her and a physical one for her husband.

Herein lies the true key to the future of the games industry. If it is really to rival other entertainment media such as the film industry, it needs to broaden its appeal. In the UK, the average age of a game player is twenty-two: 18–22 year olds make up about 32 per cent of the market, while 15–17 year olds account for a further 11 per cent, and under 14s are a further 22 per cent. A staggering 65 per cent of game players are under twenty-two. To break out of this long-held customer pattern – and make more money – the industry will need to create games that attract old and young, men and women alike. One easily notable marker of whether this is possible may be the creation of a game character which has the same sex appeal for women that Lara Croft has for men.

As for the future of how we will play games, we seem to be edging towards the sort of game activity that appears in a lot of sci-fi cyberpunk literature. Neal Stephenson's *Snowcrash*, for example, was set between the real world and a 'metaverse' in which people lived as 'avatars' – cyber-beings that exist with as much reality in cyberspace as we do in the physical universe. This vision meshes very closely with John Romero's concept of creating a game-led networked universe, containing communities of players as large as our own societies. These games would grow and evolve with time.

In these worlds, players control characters that relate to the cyber-world in much the same way as we do with the physical world; collecting history, developing character traits, making moral judgements and incurring success or failure over much longer periods of time and to varying degrees. These games raise profound questions about the nature of life, justice, family, home and community.

Anti-gamers will recoil at the thought of creating such fiendishly complex virtual worlds that compete for emotional and intellectual energy against the real world. But the physical laws that determine the advance of technology combined with the laws of human nature indicate that we are moving inexorably towards such an environment, which will eventually become an important part of daily life.

Our primeval urge to create the richest life experiences could potentially be the force that drives the gaming industry into pole position in the entertainment stakes. In any case, a quick go on *Tomb Raider* is a great deal safer than bungee jumping into the local river crevasse.

kill

Space Invaders was the first game in the virtual arms race. Released in 1978, it was also the first massive hit in the home market. Space Invaders was reason enough to buy the Atari 2600.

Space Invaders was like nothing that had come before it. Forty-eight little critters, six rows deep, edged their way towards your spaceship, firing at you. The objective was to dodge their missiles and take out their fleet. The more you shot, the faster they came. Strangely, the game had no ending; the challenge lay in getting the highest score.

Next on the scene was Asteroids. The difference with this game was that your craft was not rooted to the bottom of the screen. Instead you started in the middle, blowing away huge chunks of space debris before they hit you. Though Asteroids was released as a black-and-white game with vector graphics, many versions of it currently exist in colour on the internet. Following Asteroids came Defender, a side-scrolling shooter in which space never ended: you could keep going, dropping bombs on enemy bases, skilfully shooting flying objects.

Modern shooters are in a different league. Killing everything is still the top priority, but the player explores the environment in the first person. Your weapon is pointed out into the virtual world as if you were holding it. Some of the weapons are so big that they take up about a quarter of the screen. The plot of each game is remarkably similar: in some you still kill aliens, in others evil monsters, but most importantly you are the last person left who can save the world. Only you can do it.

The defining game in this genre is Doom, released by id Software in 1993. id Software was founded in 1990 by John Romero, John Carmack, Tom Hall and Adrian Carmack. Doom earned the kind of wealth for its creators that would make a pop star blush, and it changed the way games could be distributed. id Software gave the first two levels of the game away on the internet; the rest had to be bought. Hype for Doom started gaining pace on the US college circuit. Students were clamouring to download the game and play it on their college network (the game supported up to four people at any one time). Today, an estimated 15 million copies of Doom have been downloaded worldwide. It is available on CD-Rom, PlayStation and Nintendo. What makes it even better is that Doom can exist on an office network. This adds spice since you know the people that you are wasting.

In Doom you play a porn-loving space marine, the toughest space marine in the whole universe. You have to save the world after a science experiment goes wrong and spirits up demons from hell. As you land on the moon your colleagues are killed, and from then on the slugfest begins. You stop only to ingest various performance-enhancing drugs and pick up weapons. Despite its success, Doom is a fairly monotonous game: the character does not jump or crouch, and the tunnels the game is set in all look the same. To combat Doom fatigue, id Software released Quake in June 1996. Quake is a much better version of Doom. The player can move around more easily, and each level is bigger and has a different look.

Despite the tremendous success of id Software, Romero left in 1996 and started a new company called ION Storm with a multi-million dollar cheque from Eidos, purveyors of that fine game Tomb Raider. Romero hopes that his new release, Daikatana, will be the best-selling shooter to date. Wisely, he has chosen to break from the established mould, even though he is using id's 3D engine (the company is more than happy to license it). The game has four different levels: ancient Greece, medieval Europe, 2030 and the far future. There will be 64 different kinds of beasties to kill compared to Quake's ten, and a choice of 35 weapons. Daikatana also features a pair of talking characters to help the player. Hopefully Daikatana will be different enough to inject some new life into this rather tired gaming format. As a result of Doom's success there has been a glut of shooters including Alien Trilogy and Duke Nukem 3D. But at the end of the day Doom still reigns supreme, despite its imperfections.

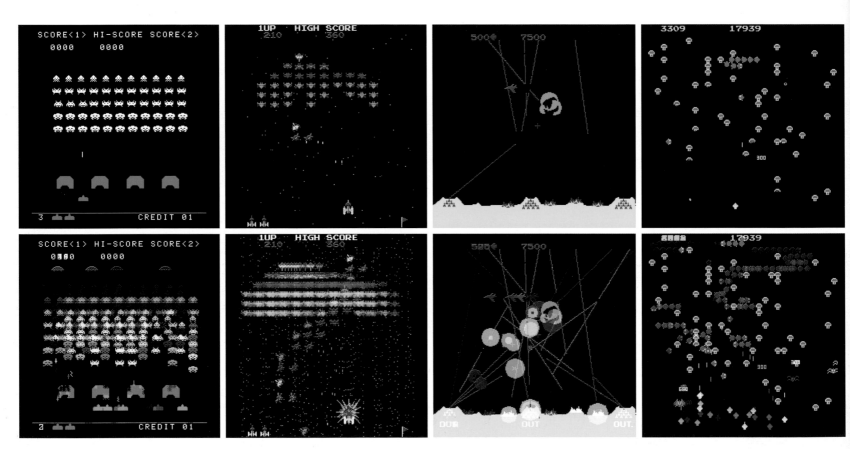

space invaders | namco | atari | arcade | 1979   galaxian | namco | atari | arcade | 1979   missile command | atari | arcade | 1980   centipede | atari | arcade | 1980

facing page [left to right, top to bottom]: 01-02 galaxian | namco | atari | 1979 | 03 moon cresta | nihon busson | arcade | 1980 | 04 missile command | atari | arcade | 1980 | 05-06 xevious | namco | arcade | 1982 | 07 blaster | williams | arcade | 1983 | 08-10 space harrier | sega | genesis | 1988 | 11-13 r-type | irem corporation | hudson soft | arcade | 1988 | 14-16 gradius 2 | konami | snes | 1990 | 17-18 phalanx | kemco | nintendo | snes | 1991 | 19-21 soldier blade | hudson soft | arcade | 1992 | 22-25 axelay | konami | nintendo | 1992 | page 22: battlezone | atari | arcade | 1980 | page 23: asteroids | atari | arcade | 1981 | page 24: star wars | atari | lucasarts | arcade | 1983 | page 25: zaxxon | sega | arcade | 1982 | page 26: defender | williams | arcade | 1980 | r-type | irem corporation | hudson soft | snes | 1988

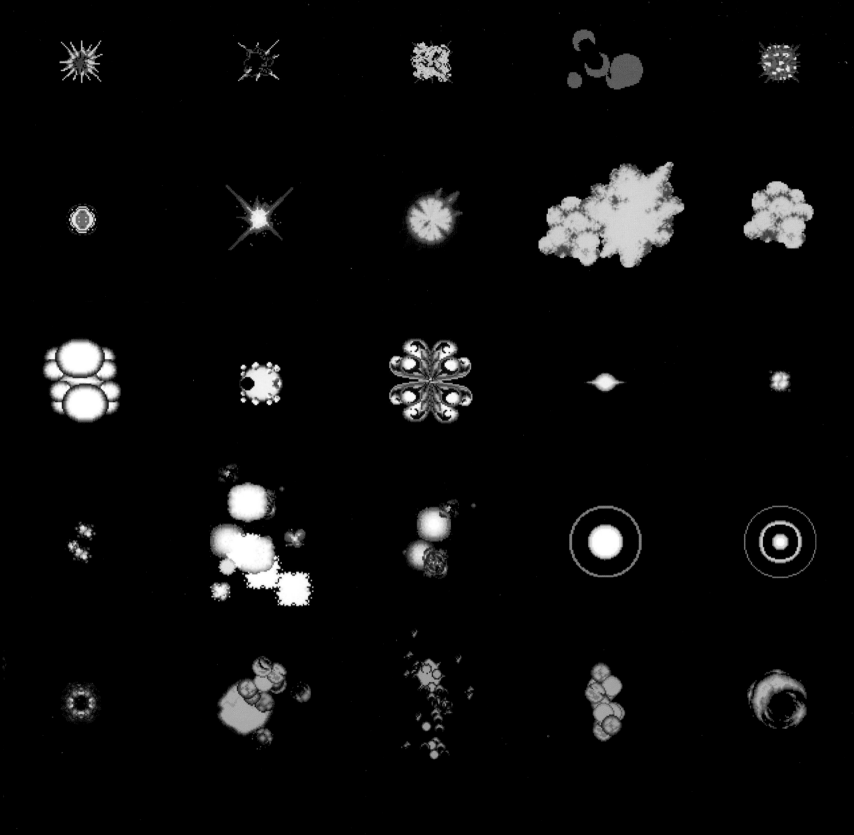

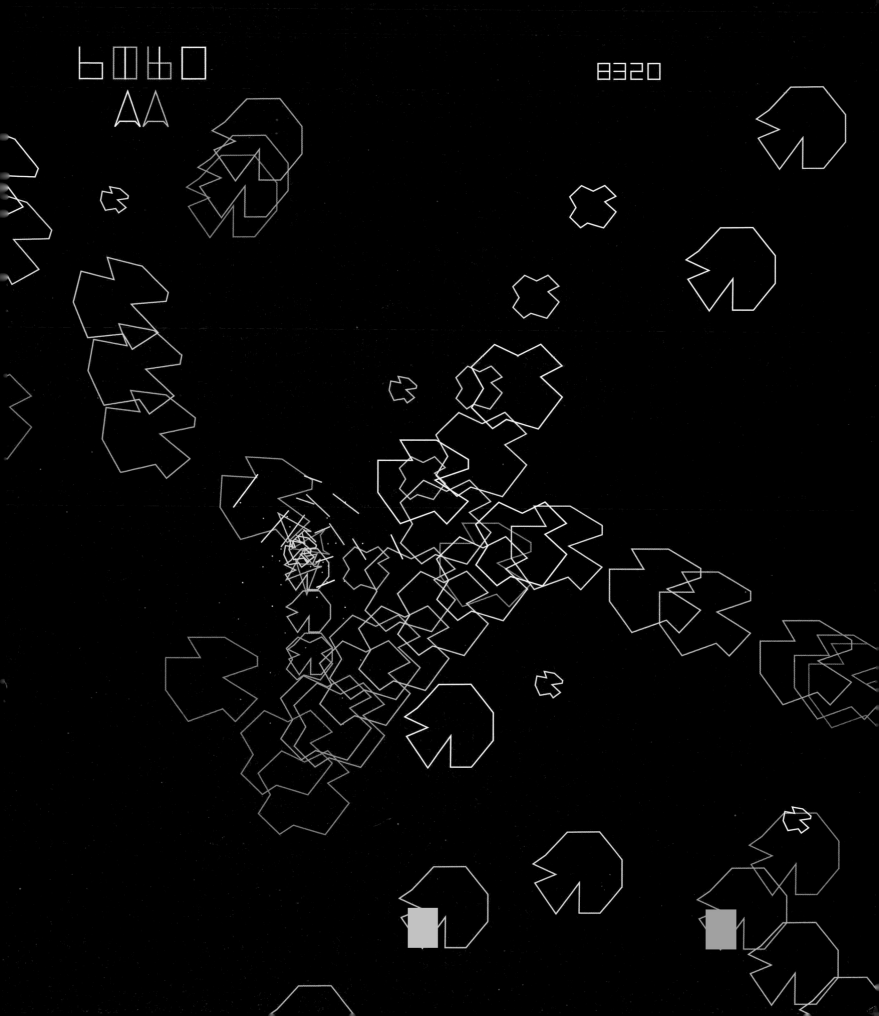

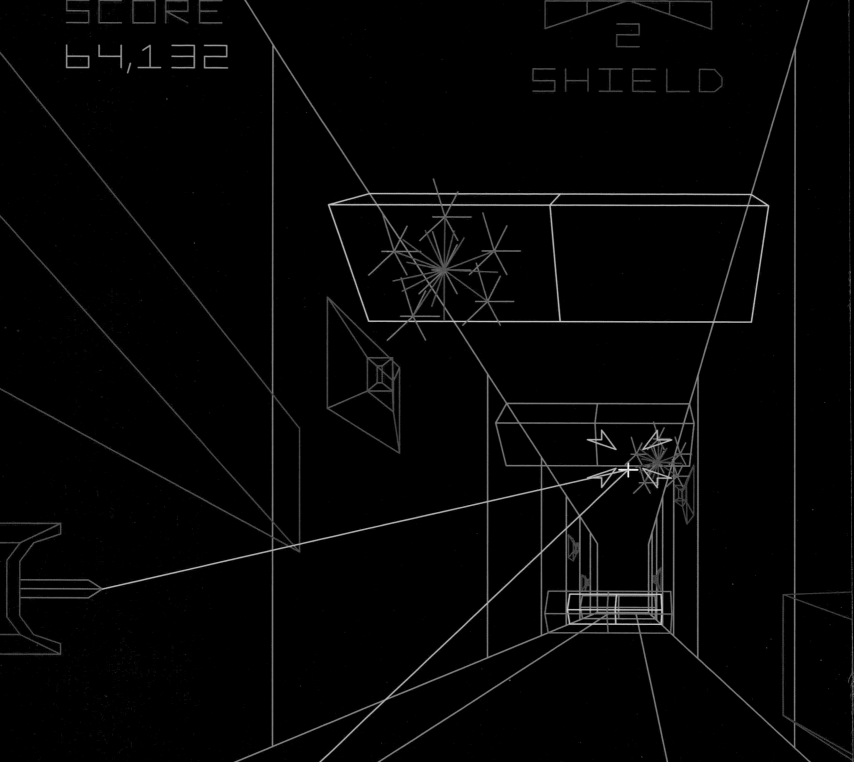

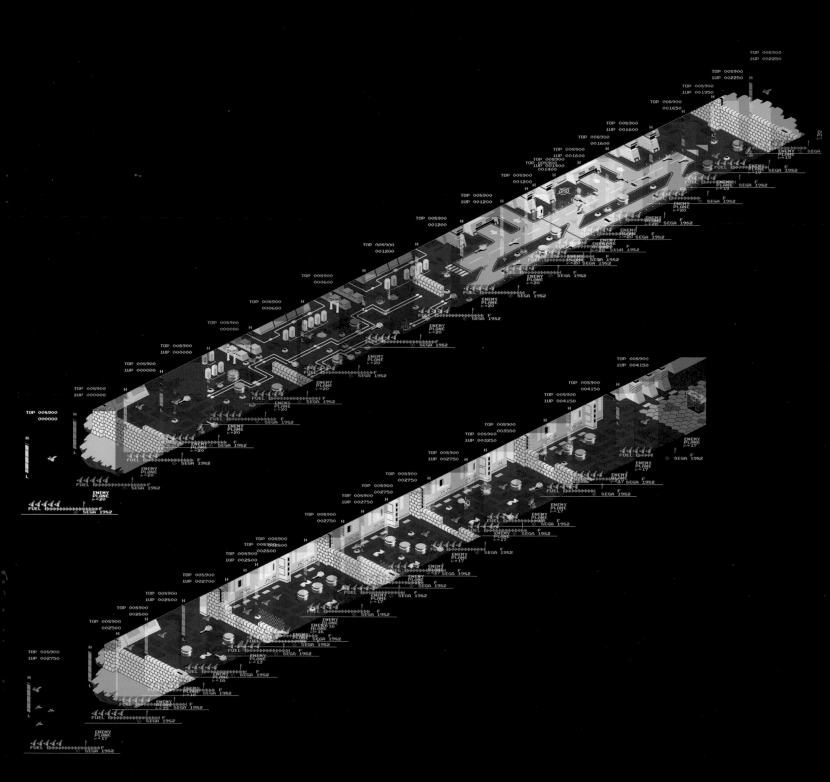

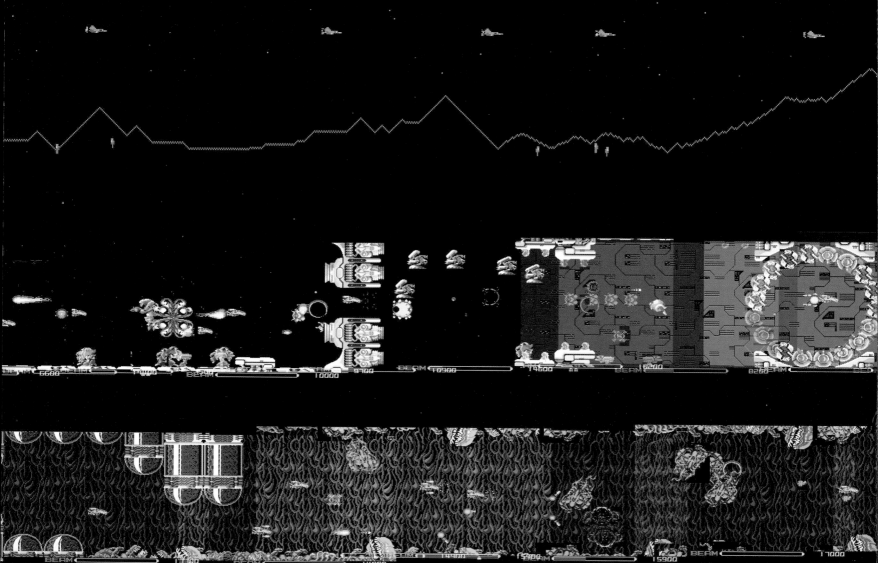

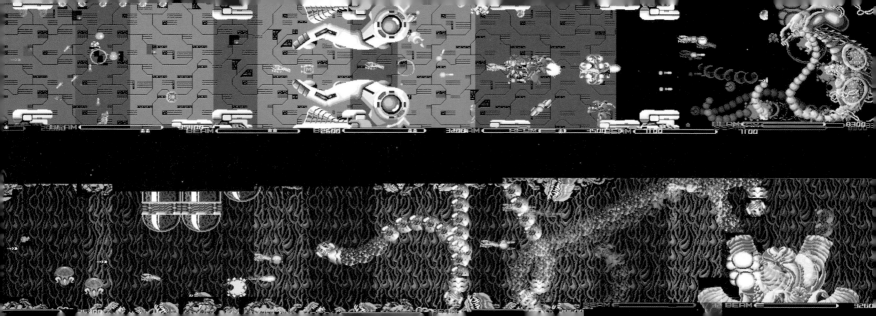

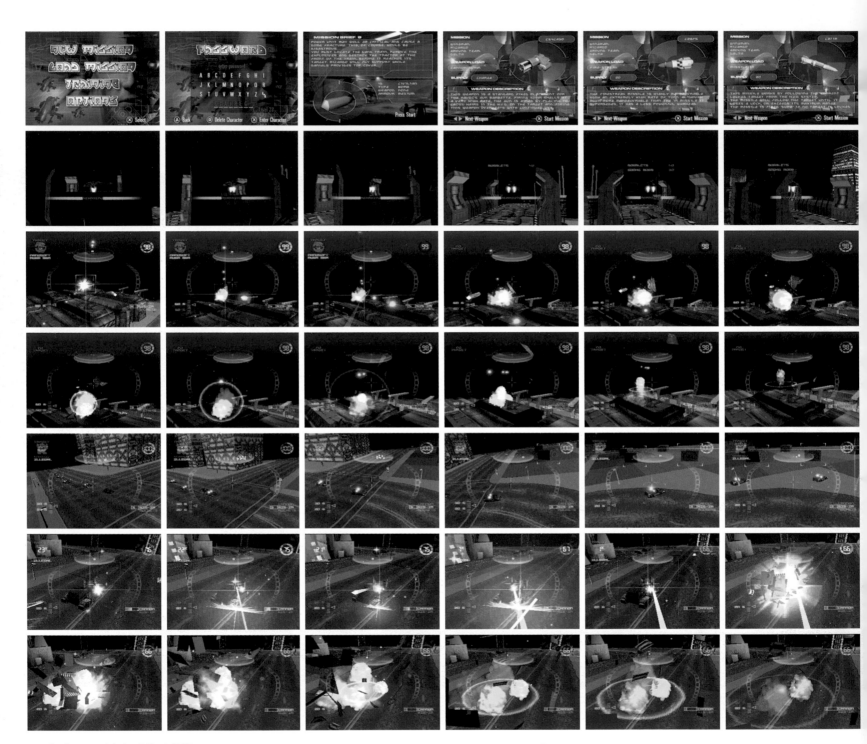

g-police | psygnosis | playstation | 1997

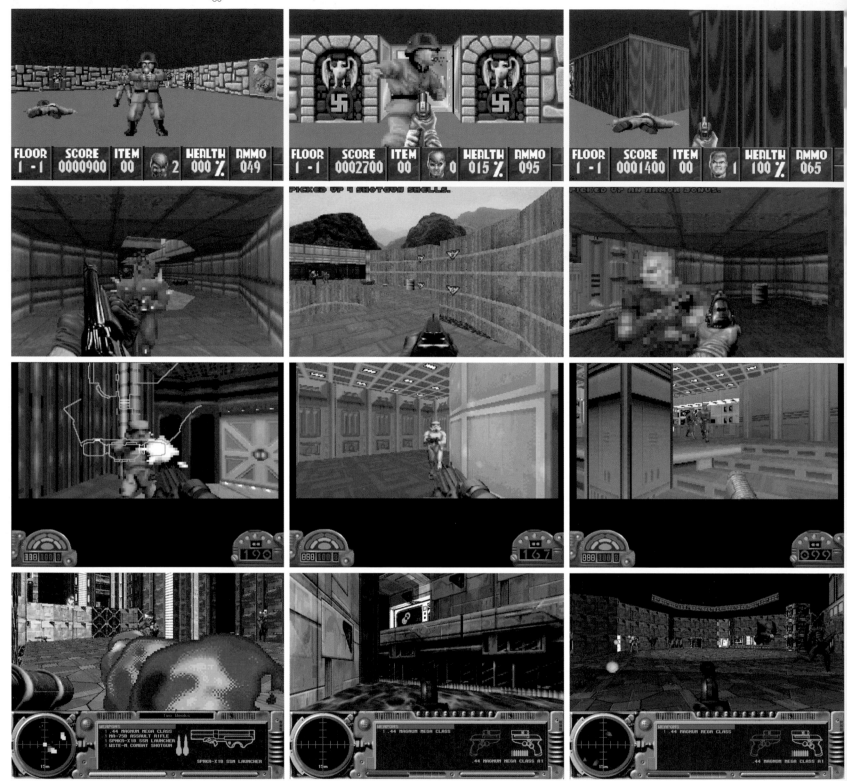

wolfenstein 3D | id | pc | 1992 | **doom** | id | pc | 1993 | **dark forces** | lucasarts | macintosh | 1995 | **marathon infinity** | bungie | macintosh | 1996

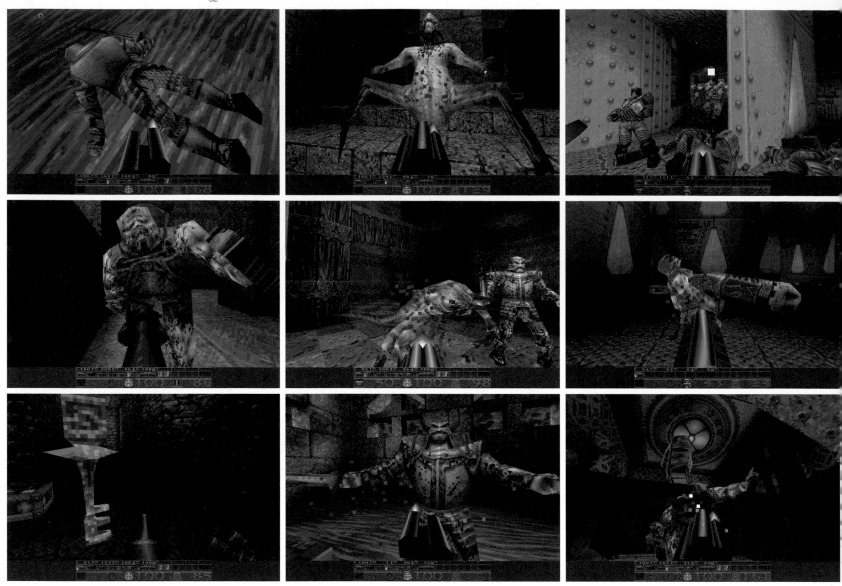

An Interview with **John Romero**, the Creator of *Doom* and *Quake*

John Romero is the godfather of computer games, the industry's guru. His life is a dream come true; his charm is that he knows this. Twenty-nine year old Romero's meteoric rise to fame and fortune is the stuff that films are made of. He never went to college or worked for a big corporation, yet his company ION Storm has been written about as one to watch in *Time* and *Fortune* magazines. By generating such interest, Romero is spreading the gospel of the industry's slacker success to big business. To symbolize this he has moved his company into the 22,000 square foot penthouse apartment of the Texas Commerce Bank building. From there Romero should have no problem attracting big investors for his new projects.

Ever since he first saw a *Pac-Man* machine in his local arcade, John Romero has been fascinated by games. Drawn into the virtual world at the age of twelve he would, to his parents' dismay, sneak out whenever possible to play. As a child he spent hours creating violent comic strips, so it comes as no surprise that he should invent the genre of the first-person 3D shoot-em-up.

Romero started to program games in high school. Each game he wrote would be named in alphabetical sequence; by the time he finished high school he had been through the alphabet twice. After leaving school he worked at Burger King and wrote games for the Apple II. He turned up on spec at the Apple II trade show in San Francisco hoping to get a job with Origin Software, and he left the show with the job he wanted. After a year at Origin, he moved to Softdisk where he met the partners with whom he would form id Software and create legendary games such as *Doom* – Tom Hall, Adrian Carmack and John Carmack. The four worked together at Softdisk until the launch of their first title, *Commander Keen*, which was released in December 1990. One month later they left to form id

Software. On May 5 1992, id hit the big time with its revolutionary game *Wolfenstein 3D*. This game launched the genre of first-person 3D shooters which remains popular today. id's 3D engine dramatically raised the expectations of gamers. Over 250,000 copies of the game were sold and millions of gamers have played the shareware version.

On December 10 1993, id Software went down in gaming history when it released *Doom*. *Doom* is recognized as a classic. It was released as a shareware game, and millions of copies have been downloaded. *Doom II* followed shortly afterwards. In his spare time Romero oversaw production of Raven Software's *Heretic* and *Hexen* before working on id's blockbuster game *Quake*, released in 1996. Pre-orders for this game exceeded 750,000. *Quake* was an improved version of *Doom*, involving more levels, more monsters and better character movement. When *Quake II* was released in December 1997 it was hailed by many industry magazines around the world as the best computer game ever. Despite its phenomenal success, however, Romero was at loggerheads with id company policy. While John Carmack, the programmer and creator of the 3D engine, favoured producing one game a year, Romero felt he could release several different versions of a game in a year. He accepted a $13 million advance from Eidos Technologies and set up his own company ION Storm.

His first release through ION Storm is *Daikatana*, which represents a move away from his usual blood fest. Although the game is still gory, Romero has added better graphics, music, sound and monsters. The game also has four different time periods so the player does not get bored. A major feature of *Daikatana* is that the player journeys through the game with the help of two computer-controlled characters. It's a bold move, and the eyes of the industry are on ION Storm.

quake | id | pc + macintosh | 1996

What inspirations and influences led you to create Wolfenstein 3D?
Well, first off I'd have to say the original Apple II *Castle Wolfenstein* game by Muse Software that was released in 1981. For our first mainstream 3D engine game we wanted to do something really different, so the idea of escaping from a Nazi castle during World War II and blowing away guards seemed like a very novel setting.

What comes first when you prepare a game, the story or the graphic look?
The story comes first.

The success of your games has led to many imitators. How do you feel about this and has anyone bettered you?
I love playing other great 3D games and am very happy with the results of many of them such as *Duke 3D*, *Dark Forces*, *Jedi Knight* and *Blood*. I definitely believe that *Duke 3D* and *Dark Forces* were on a par with my past games and in many areas were even better.

How will your new games differ from those that have come before them?
Content and a strong adherence to the storyline. Every part of *Daikatana* should feel fresh and new, from the level itself to the monsters, music, sound effects, weapons, you name it. It's all different every step of the way.

You have hired Christian Divine to direct the characters in *Daikatana*. What do you think is the secret to creating successful on-screen characters and why have so many people failed to do so in the past?
Characterization is the key to creating memorable characters: when you strongly support your story in the game you can really spend time on the backgrounds and motivations of the characters which makes them memorable and in turn makes your game memorable.

Would you ever consider producing a different genre of game?
Sure, I'm always interested in other genres but right now I believe I'll stick to what I am best at and that's first-person 3D games.

Do you believe that the violence of some computer games has a destructive influence on society?
Violent games might produce a bad side-effect in unstable individuals but overall I believe that violent games are a good thing because they provide a release for built-up stress and tension.

What single thing do you think could improve the experience of gameplay? In ten years' time what new experiences do you think games will be able to offer the player?
I don't think that one particular thing will improve your gaming experience – all the tiny details are usually what end up making the player feel very good overall about a game. In ten years who knows what's going to happen? There might be entirely new genres created or we might all be making games on a single 4D super engine.

What constitutes a great game?
A great game gets a strong emotional reaction from the player. It's that simple.

What other games do you enjoy playing?
I really love all of Squaresoft's games, especially the *Final Fantasy* series and *Chrono Trigger*. *Age of Empires* by Ensemble Studios is an awesome real-time strategy game that I love playing. Right now though, I've been playing a lot of *Doom II*.

goldeneye | rare | nintendo | n64 | 1997

PICKED UP A D5K DEUTSCHE.

8 | 30

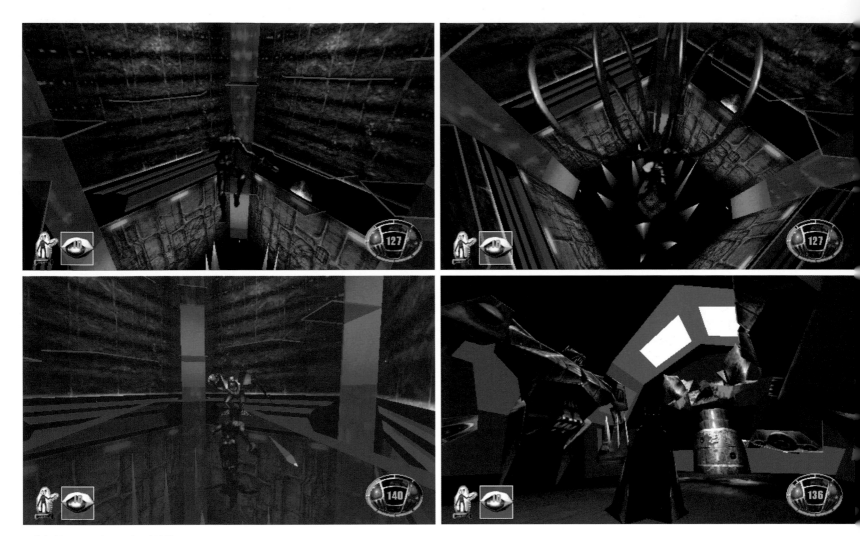

mdk | shiny entertainment | pc | 1997

turok: dinosaur hunter | acclaim | n64 | 1997

Sports games manufacturers never miss an opportunity to sell a game. Olympics, Super Bowls, World Cups – you name it, they will make it. As a result there are dozens of terrible games on the market for every sporting discipline: golf, baseball, football, fishing, basketball, bowling, even deer hunting.

At the heart of sports games are celebrity endorsements, a clever way to earn players more money and with any luck make a game more marketable. Titles include *Alan Shearer Actua Soccer*, *Jack Nicklaus Golf* and *Pete Sampras Tennis*. Securing a number one professional for a game is one thing, but it will not ensure success. As it takes over a year to produce a game, the trick is to choose someone who will still be hot at the time of release; sudden deaths, disqualifications, injuries or a horrendous lack of form can spell disaster for a game.

Until recently, simulating any sport apart from tennis was futile. Today, however, technology has come so far that it is actually possible to recreate something similar to what you see when you watch a match on television. This is thanks to a technique called motion capture which is used to create convincing human movement for both film and games. The motion capture system was developed by Oxford Metric and was used originally in the medical world to analyse gait. Now they are moving into entertainment, Oxford Metric are one of the leading companies in motion capture. The technology allows characters realistic 3D movement within a game's environment, making gameplay convincing and addictive.

England striker Les Ferdinand had to perform a gruelling 202 moves to be captured for an Eidos soccer game. The game's creators devised these moves by looking at those in other titles on the market and then adding more. Captures for the game also include player celebrations – such as Lee Sharp's Elvis impersonation – making fun of the referee when his back is turned and even a punch-up.

The data collected from Ferdinand was used as the basis for movement for every character in the game, including the referee and the goalkeeper. The data was then individually tailored to each player depending on their height and weight. The idea is to capture lots of random motions and then edit them together, for example, combining a run and a kick so that in the end the animation flows constantly.

Though most motion capture data is gathered in a studio, some has to be gathered outside – a sliding tackle could cause quite a carpet burn. Motion capture works using seven wide-angle cameras set up in a ring. Coordinates are set so that each camera knows exactly where it is in the space. All the cameras are plugged into a standard PC, and each processes sixty frames a second. The subject is covered in thirty reflective balls, which act as markers, detected by the computer in each frame from each camera. The information is triangulated by the computer, and the subject's movement in 3D space is established.

After the data has been collected, each marker in every capture has to be labelled by hand. This is so the computer knows where the front of the head is, and so on. When this has been done the sequences are cleaned up, and any missing markers that might have been obstructed are added. The final process is to create an Acclaim File. There are two types: an ASF, which gives details of the skeleton, such as the number and length of bones; and an AMC file, which gives the angle of the joints in each capture. The files can then be exported into Alias or SoftImage before they are attached to a body. Put it all together and you have a sports game based around the real movements of a premiership player.

It could be argued that sport was the first genre of interactive games as *Pong* is a version of tennis. Though change was a long time coming, creating realistic human movement has revolutionized the games market. Sports sims such as Electronic Arts' *NHL Hockey* and Gremlin's *Actua* series are redefining sports games as one of the industry's most cutting-edge genres.

winter heat | sega | saturn | 1998

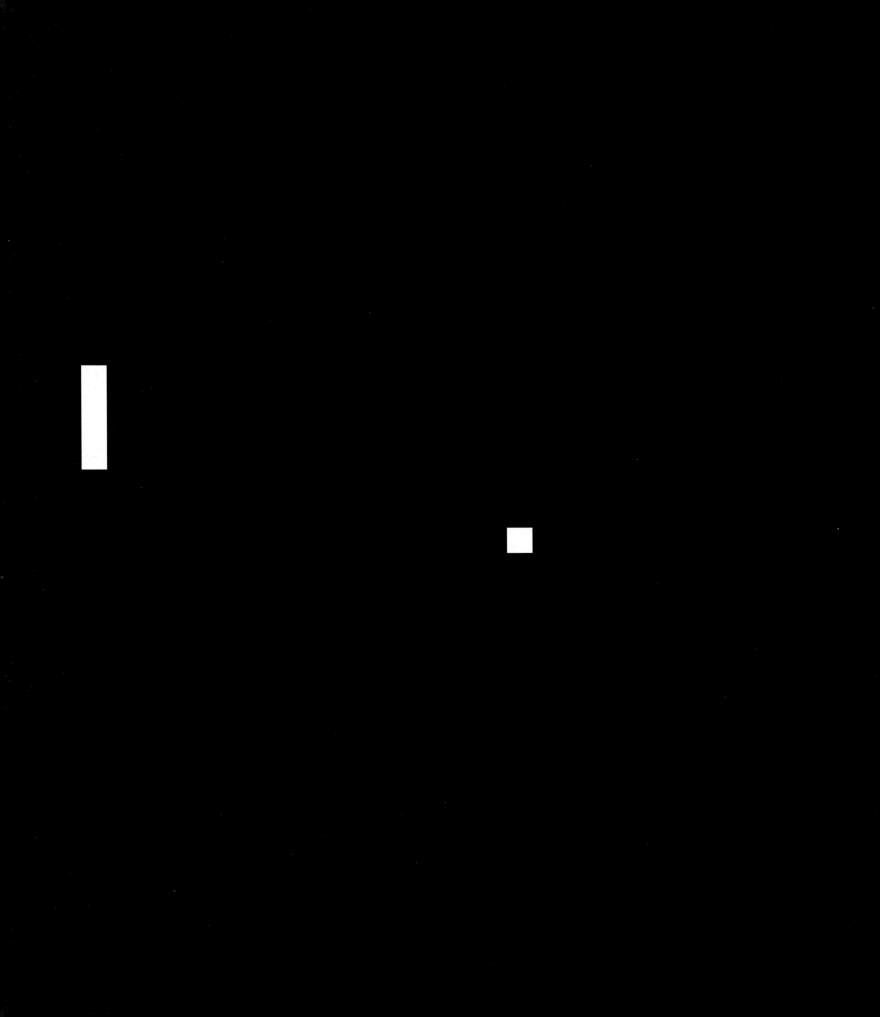

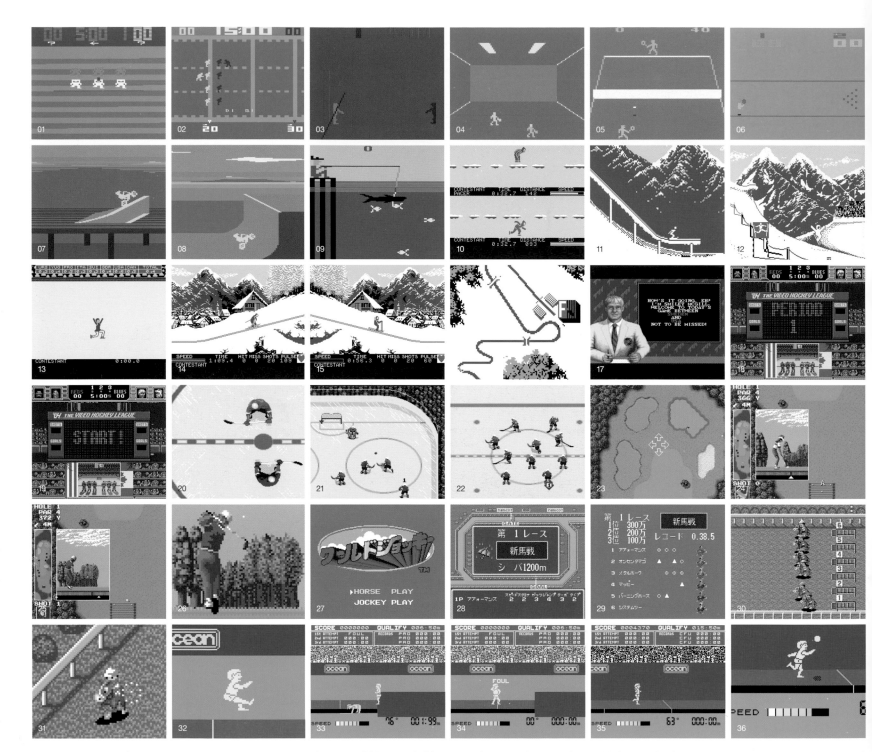

01 football | atari 2600 | 02 super football | atari 2600 | 03 basketball | atari 2600 | 04 racquetball | atari 2600 | 05 tennis | activision | atari 2600 | 06 bowling | atari 2600 | 07-08 bmx air master | sculptured software, tnt | atari 2600 | 1989 | 09 fishing derby | activision | atari 2600 | 10-16 winter games | us gold, epyx | spectrum | 17-22 tv sports hockey | nec | pc engine | 1991 | 23-26 power golf | hudson soft | pc engine | 1989 | 27-31 horse racing | namco | pc engine | 1991 | 32-36 daley thompson's decathlon | ocean | spectrum | 1985 | 37-41 super baseball simulator 1000 | culture brain usa inc | snes | 1991 | 42-45 3d tennis | spectrum | 46-48 summer games 3 | epyx | c64 | 1985 | 49-56 california games | epyx | milton bradley | nes | 1985 | 57-58 ping-pong | konami | msx | 1985 | 59-60 speedball 2 | imageworks | 61-64 world court tennis | namco | nec | pc engine | 1989 | 65-69 soccer | konami | msx | 1985 | 70-72 super tennis | tokyo shoseki | nintendo | snes | 1991

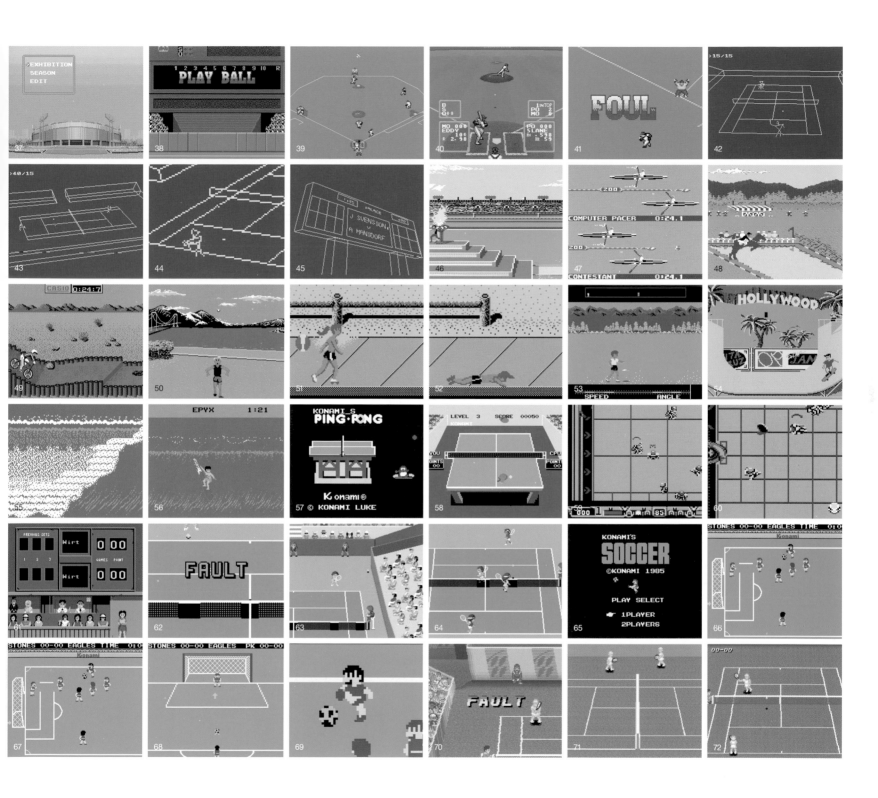

winter heat | sega | saturn | 1998

1080° snowboarding | nintendo | n64 | 1998

nhl **98** | ea sports | pc | 1998

actua soccer | gremlin interactive | pc | 1997

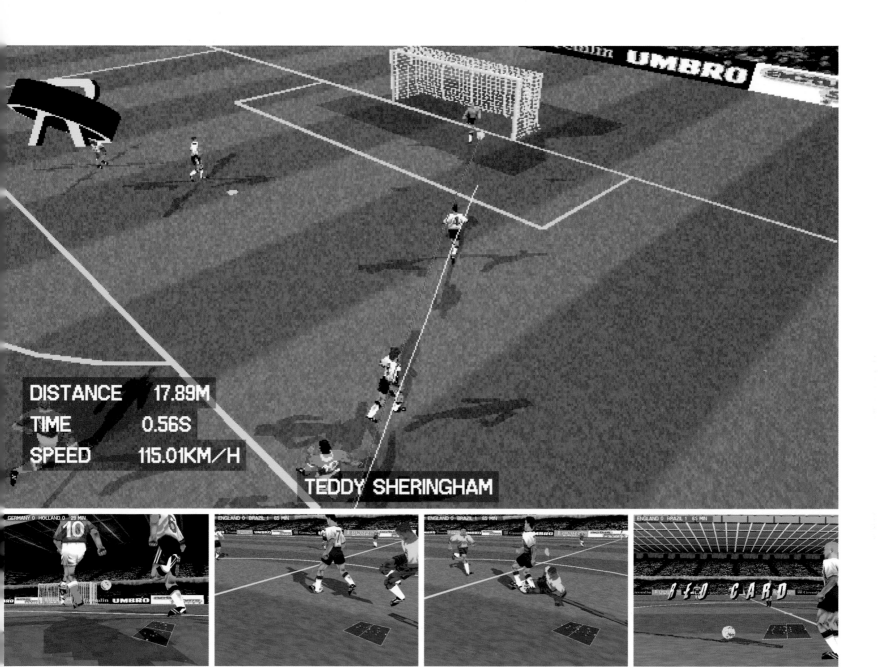

DISTANCE 17.89M

TIME 0.56S

SPEED 115.01KM/H

TEDDY SHERINGHAM

GERMANY 0 HOLLAND 0 29 MIN

ENGLAND 0 BRAZIL 1 65 MIN

ENGLAND 0 BRAZIL 1 65 MIN

ENGLAND 0 BRAZIL 1 65 MIN

RED CARD

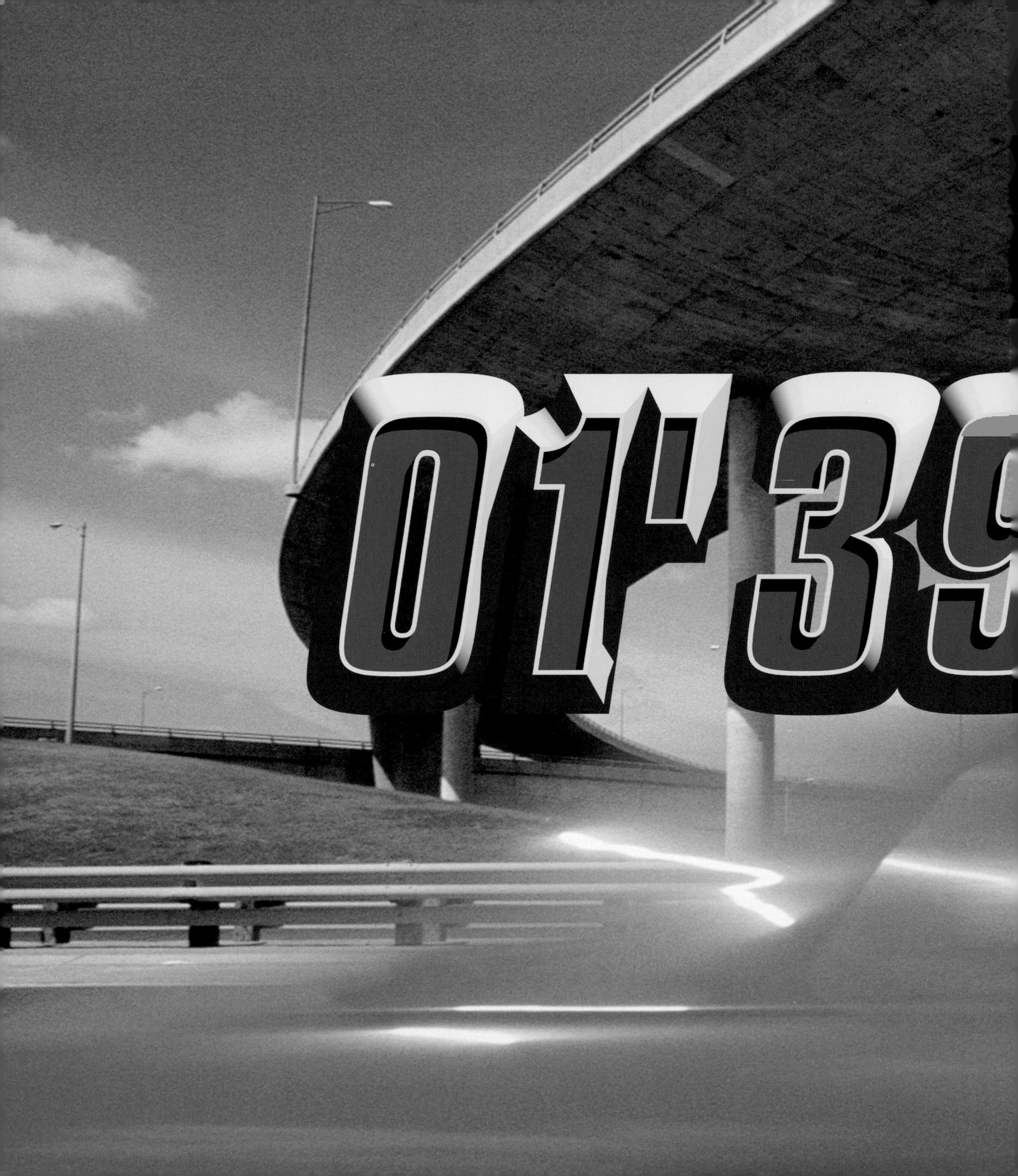
01' 3

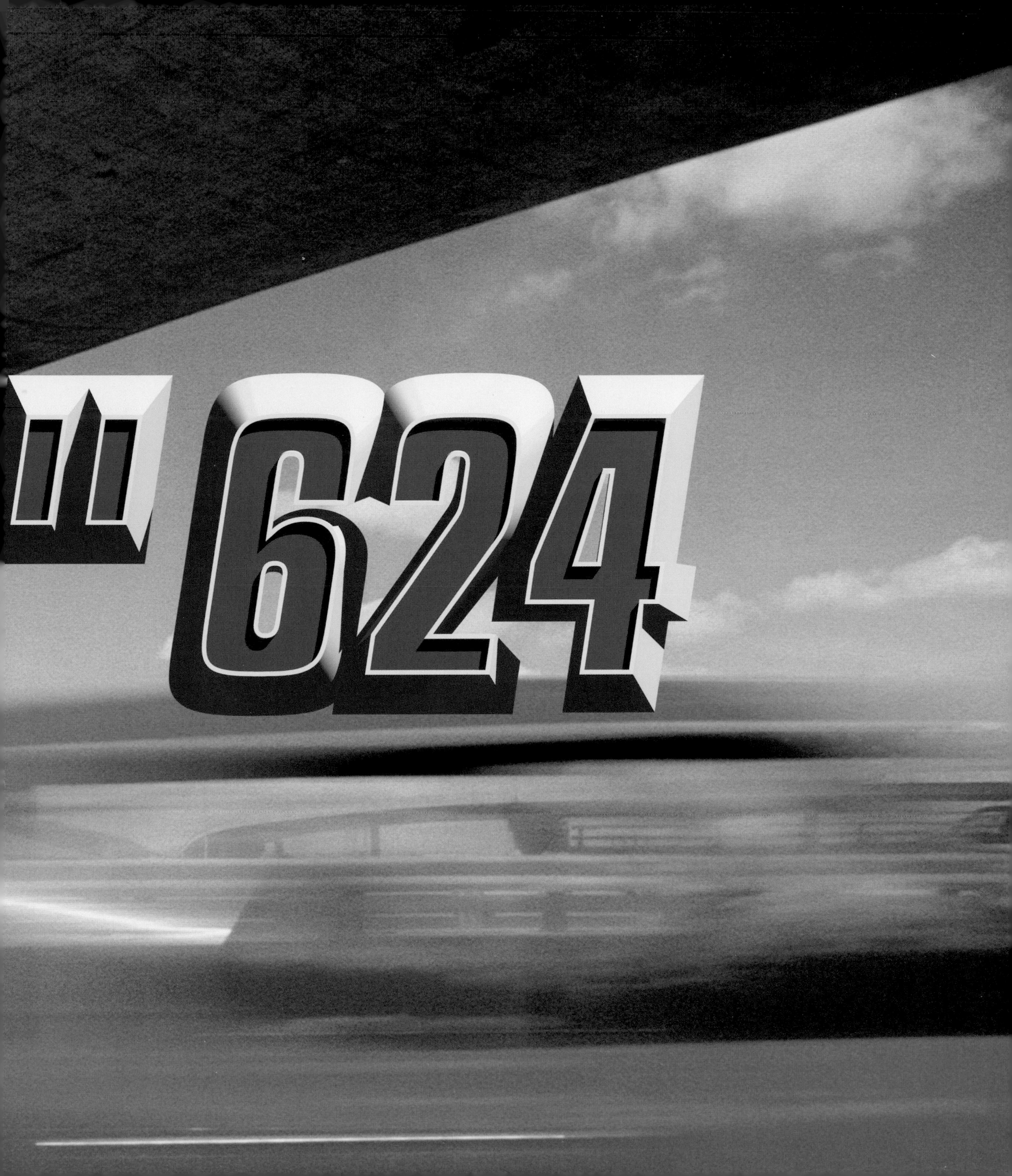
"624

drive

In the old days the best driving simulations were housed in local arcades as players really needed a steering wheel, gears and accelerator to believe they were racing in a Grand Prix – the hand-held controls and 'few-bit' graphics of a home console were not quite the same.

Today, popular driving games such as *Formula 1*, *Pole Position* and *Ridge Racer* sell very well indeed, and no serious games collection is complete without a driving game or two. Since driving games tend to be rather repetitive, developers have recently sought to spice up the gameplay by making it more violent (games such as *Carmageddon* and *Destruction Derby* are good examples). In these games the objective is not only to win but to batter your opponents.

Then in 1998 Polys Entertainment released *Gran Turismo*. This game is billed as the 'real driving simulator' and it certainly lives up to its name; it is the ultimate racer. The full-motion graphics of the intro sequence are astounding, and the beauty of *Gran Turismo* is that the graphics of the game proper are almost as stunning. For the first time in the history of driving games, the best graphics are available in the home and not on a coin-op in the arcade. The detail is amazing – the cars actually reflect the environment they are placed in: as you zoom around the track it is possible to see the hoardings in the paintwork.

Nearly 300 cars from ten different manufacturers are available to the player, and each vehicle has independent four-wheel suspension. The double stroke of genius is that Polys Entertainment has added real depth to the gameplay. The player's goal is still to be the fastest round the circuit, but the best vehicles and most glamorous races are not immediately accessible. A player begins the game as a novice with a second-hand car and works their way up. As they compete they earn prize money which enables them to buy a better car. Players must also obtain a license; a B license is earned through driving in the Sunday Cup; they can then progress to an A license which allows the real racing to begin.

It is certain that after the launch of *Gran Turismo* developers around the world abandoned the driving games they were working on and went back to the drawing board; Polys Entertainment not only moved the goal posts, they placed them out of sight.

gran turismo | scee (polys entertainment) | playstation | 1998

01-04 pole position | atari | atari 2600 | 1983 | 05-09 rally x | midway | arcade | 1980 | 10-11 fatal run | atari | atari 2600 | 1989 | 12-16 buggy boy | taito | tatsumi | c64 | 1987 | 17-21 roadblaster | atari | arcade | 1986 | 22-25 roadfighter | konami | msx | 1985 | 26-28 demolition derby | bally | midway | arcade | 1984 | 29-32 outrun | ikari | c64 | 1987 | 33-36 lombard rally | red rat | mandarin | atari st | 1988

pole position | atari | namco | zx spectrum | 1983

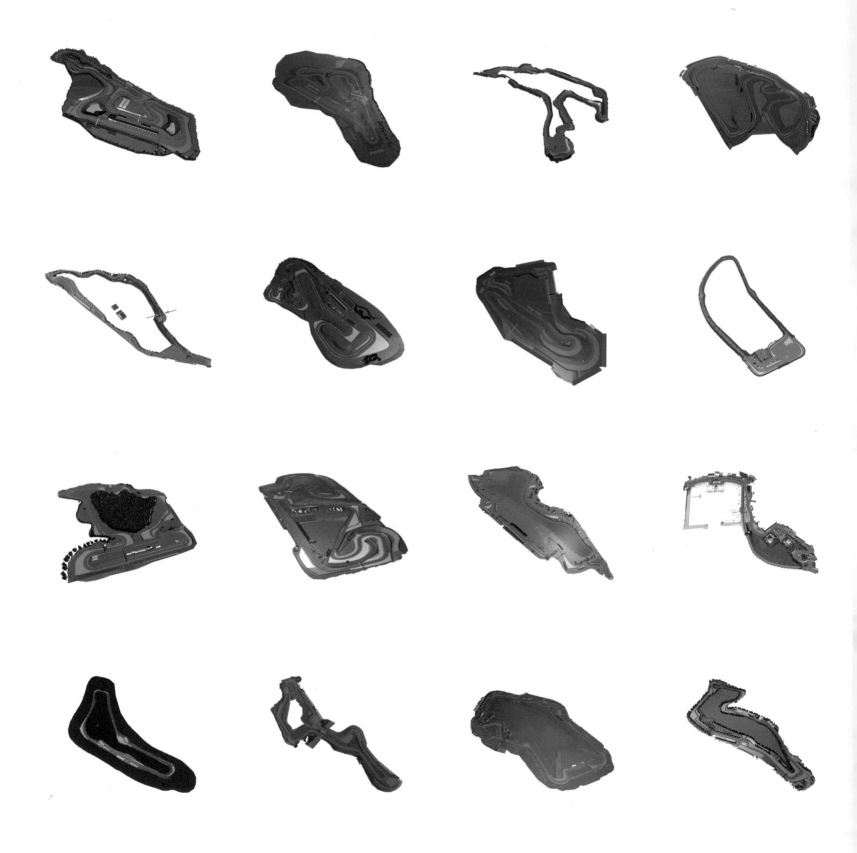

formula 1 '97 | psygnosis | playstation | 1997

formula 1 '97 | psygnosis | playstation | 1997

f1 racing simulation | ubisoft | playstation | 1998

super mario kart | nintendo + rare | n64 | 1996

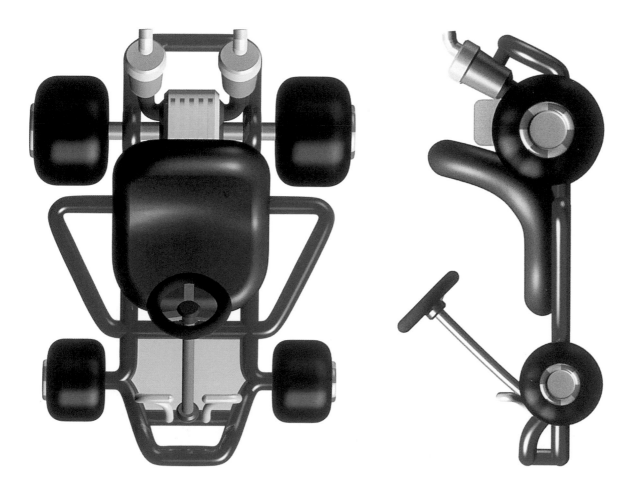

super mario kart | nintendo + rare | n64 | 1996

wipeout 2097 | psygnosis | playstation | 1996

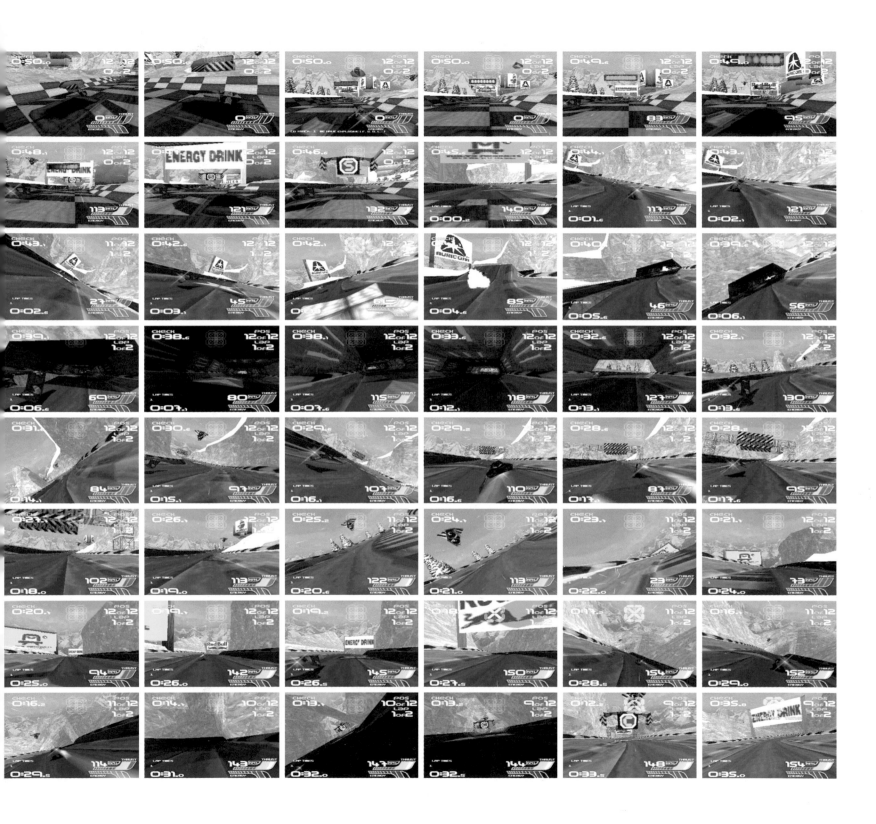

gran turismo | scee (polys entertainment) | playstation | 1998

explore

This section covers three genres of games: adventure, role playing games (RPG) and platform. We have chosen to group these together under the title Explore as over the last few years there has been a noticeable convergence of the three genres.

Platform is the largest market for home entertainment games. In 1982 Colecovision (later to become Nintendo) released *Donkey Kong*. The objective of the game was simple: to rescue Princess Daisy from the grasp of a large gorilla; its unlikely star was an Italian plumber called Mario.

Donkey Kong set a precedent for the style and format of platform games that is still followed today. The only real difference is that the graphics now are 3D, not 2D. The challenges remain the same, namely jumping to avoid things, jumping over gaps on the platforms and picking things up to acquire extra lives. In a platform game a player cannot get off the route, they have to travel a set course. As a result of *Donkey Kong*, home entertainment became big business very quickly.

Nine years after Mario's first appearance Sega introduced its spiky mascot *Sonic the Hedgehog*. Sonic and Mario were pitted in a head-to-head conflict. Yet despite the politics of big business, it is the market that judges the games. More recent releases such as PlayStation's *Pandemonium* and *Crash Bandicoot* follow an established format yet still become big hits. Each developer is constantly striving to find another character that will capture the imagination in a platform format. In the meantime they make do with adopting characters from the big screen – such as *Robocop* and *Jurassic Park*'s dinosaurs – to little effect.

Though platform games can in this day and age seem somewhat dull, repeating a task and succeeding becomes a very personal vendetta. Play is obsessive as no one wants to be defeated by the game. To be good at platform a player needs timing, fast reflexes and patience. The bulk of games, however, are set in cutesy, cartoon-like worlds. They are really games for children that adults can enjoy.

Fortunately the programmers' wish to build up complex, intricate worlds, coupled with the boom in home computer sales, brought about a boom in adult-targeted games. The extra memory of the personal computer was able to reproduce far superior graphics, yet it lacked the speed of a console. It lent itself to adventure-style games. Adventure games have existed for years, often in text-only format, for example *Dungeons and Dragons*. CD-Rom adventure games allow the player to explore an environment in the first person at their own pace. Navigation is via the cursor point, click and drag.

Undoubtedly the best games graphics in this genre were created by brothers Robyn and Rand Miller, whose 1993 release *Myst* transcended everything that had come before it. Their follow-up, *Riven*, was even more beautiful. Released on CD-Rom in 1997, it was a huge, memory-hungry game played over five disks. *Riven* required 75 megabytes of hard-disk space, a four-speed CD-Rom drive and a recommended 35 megabytes of memory. The results, breathtaking ray-traced images, occupy the whole screen, enabling the player to become fully immersed in this strange mechanical land. Spectacular full motion video appears without warning. These games are not easy to master. Some players are left confused and frustrated by the intricate gameplay and complex puzzle-solving. Nevertheless, the games do tell a great tale.

Role playing games achieve a balance between the highly complex puzzle-solving of adventure games and the action and characters of the platform genre. The characters are free to explore their virtual world, while performing a series of complex acrobatics, killing and puzzle-solving. Realistically human characters replace blue hedgehogs. The most famous of these polygon characters is Lara Croft, an empowered female character born with a silver spoon in her mouth. She burst on to the scene in 1996, star of the *Indiana Jones*-style game *Tomb Raider*, a tension-packed shooter with puzzles, obstacles and, best of all, underwater swimming. Lara Croft captured players' imaginations; despite being only a virtual babe she has acquired celebrity status (see page 90).

Pushing the barriers of this genre, though not to everybody's taste, is Squaresoft's RPG extravaganza *Final Fantasy VII*, released in 1997. The advertising hype which commenced well before the game's release came good. With an estimated hundred hours of gameplay, *FFVII* incorporates battles, complex puzzles and magic, with character interaction. The game has jaw-dropping graphics, polygon characters set in front of breathtaking 2D backdrops. For the first time, fully rendered computer animation is seamlessly integrated into the game with no loading time whatsoever. *FFVII* has the added bonus of an excellent plot worthy of any adventure game, centring around Cloud, an ex-soldier who joins a rebel group to save the world. The character's success in the game is predetermined by decisions you have already made. Games like these are out of the league of the younger gamer. The future is already here.

facing page: final fantasy 7 | squaresoft | eidos | playstation | 1997
page 72: pac-man | midway | arcade | 1980 | page 73: frogger | sega | arcade 1982

PAC-MAN

READY!

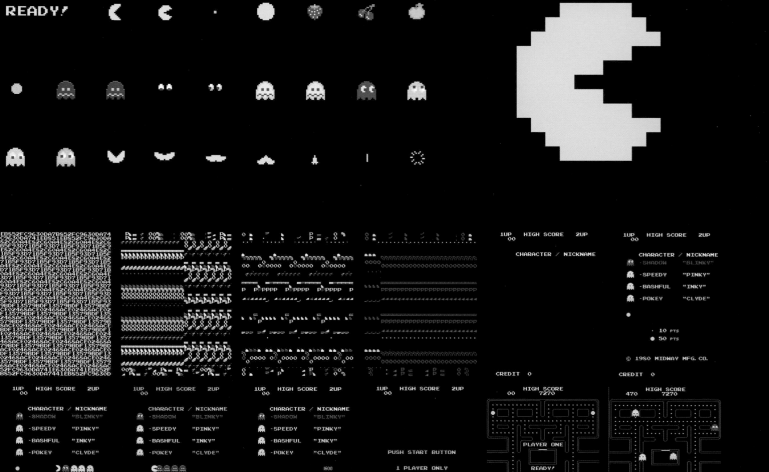

1UP   HIGH SCORE   2UP
 00

CHARACTER / NICKNAME

-SHADOW   "BLINKY"
-SPEEDY   "PINKY"
-BASHFUL   "INKY"
-POKEY   "CLYDE"

· 10 PTS
● 50 PTS

© 1980 MIDWAY MFG. CO.

CREDIT 0

1UP   HIGH SCORE   2UP
 00

CHARACTER / NICKNAME

-SHADOW   "BLINKY"
-SPEEDY   "PINKY"
-BASHFUL   "INKY"
-POKEY   "CLYDE"

· 10 PTS
● 50 PTS

© 1980 MIDWAY MFG. CO.

CREDIT 0

1UP   HIGH SCORE   2UP
 00

CHARACTER / NICKNAME

-SHADOW   "BLINKY"
-SPEEDY   "PINKY"
-BASHFUL   "INKY"
-POKEY   "CLYDE"

· 10 PTS
50 PTS

© 1980 MIDWAY MFG. CO.

CREDIT 0

1UP   HIGH SCORE   2UP
 00

CHARACTER / NICKNAME

-SHADOW   "BLINKY"
-SPEEDY   "PINKY"
-BASHFUL   "INKY"
-POKEY   "CLYDE"

                    1600

· 10 PTS
● 50 PTS

© 1980 MIDWAY MFG. CO.

CREDIT 0

1UP   HIGH SCORE   2UP
 00

PUSH START BUTTON

1 PLAYER ONLY

BONUS PAC-MAN FOR 10000 PTS

© 1980 MIDWAY MFG. CO.

CREDIT 1

        HIGH SCORE
 00   7270

PLAYER ONE

READY!

        HIGH SCORE
 470   7270

F R O G G E R

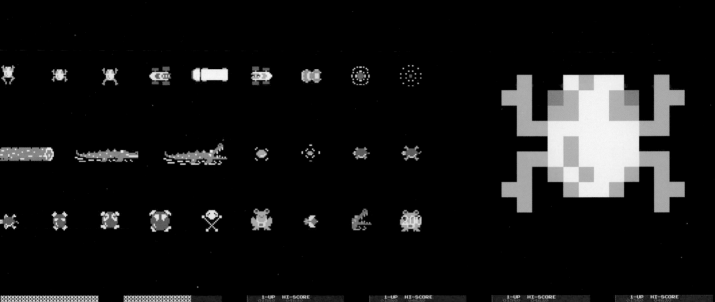

1-UP HI-SCORE
01580 04630

F R O G * * *

CREDIT 00

1-UP HI-SCORE
01580 04630

F R O G G E R

CREDIT 00

FROGGER

MOVE FROG VERTICALLY OR
HORIZONTALLY USING JOYSTICK

OBJECT IS TO SAFELY
MANEUVER FROG TO HIS HOME
WITHOUT ALLOTTED TIME
-SIXTY BEATS ON THE TIMER-

CROSS HIGHWAY WITHOUT
GETTING RUN OVER AND
CROSS RIVER WITHOUT
FALLING IN

AVOID TRAFFIC DEADLY
SNAKES OTTERS CROCODILES
AND THE TREACHEROUS
DIVING TURTLES

POINTS ARE SCORED
FOR EACH SAFE JUMP
-10 POINTS-

SAFELY ARRIVING HOME
-50 POINTS-

AND FOR BEATING THE TIMER
-10 POINTS PER BEAT SAVED-

BONUS POINTS ARE SCORED
BY ESCORTING HOME
A LADY FROG
-200 POINTS-

GOBBLING AN INSECT
-200 POINTS-

AND SAFELY GETTING
ALL FIVE FROGS HOME
-1000 POINTS-

1-UP HI-SCORE
01580 04630

SCORE RANKING

1 ST   04630 PTS
2 ND   02050 PTS
3 RD   01970 PTS
4 TH   01580 PTS
5 TH   01270 PTS

1-UP HI-SCORE
01580 04630

INSERT COIN

3 FROGS PER PLAYER

1-UP HI-SCORE
01580 04630

PUSH

START BUTTON

ONE PLAYER ONLY

ONE EXTRA FROG 20000 PTS

1-UP HI-SCORE
01580 04630

CREDIT 00   CREDIT 00   CREDIT 00   CREDIT 00   CREDIT 01   TIME

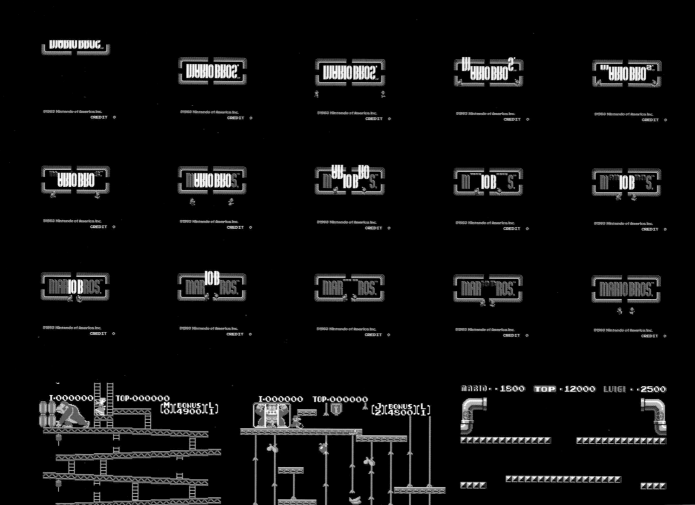

lakitu bros.
super mario rpg

yoshi
yoshi's island
super mario rpg
yoshi's story

bowser
super mario bros.
super mario world
super mario 64

boshi
super mario rpg

shy guy
yoshi's island

baby bowser
yoshi's story

poochie
yoshi's island

mario
donkey kong
donkey kong jr.
mario bros.
super mario bros.
super mario bros. 2
super mario bros. 3
super mario land
super mario land 2
super mario world
yoshi's island
super mario rpg
super mario 64

dixie kong
donkey kong country

donkey kong
donkey kong
donkey kong junior
donkey kong country 1
donkey kong country 2
donkey kong country 3

princess
mario bros.
super mario bros.
super mario bros. 2
super mario bros. 3
super mario land 2
super mario rpg
super mario 64

pauline
donkey kong

wario
super mario land 2
wario land
wario's woods
wario blast
virtual boy wario land

luigi
mario bros.

diddy kong
donkey kong country
donkey kong country 2
donkey kong country 3

nintendo family tree [background: super mario bros. | nintendo | nes | 1986] | facing page: donkey kong | nintendo | nes | 1981 | donkey kong jr. | nintendo | nes | 1982 | mario bros. | nintendo | nes| 1983

super mario world | nintendo | snes | 1991

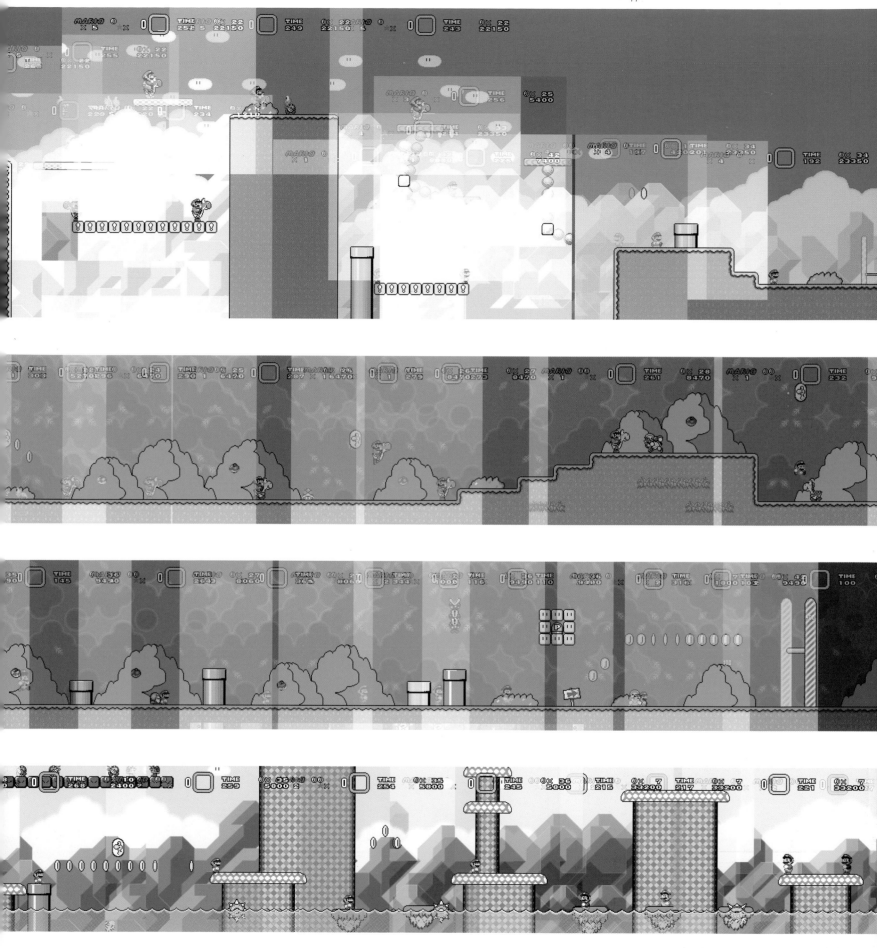

super mario 64 | nintendo | n64 | 1996

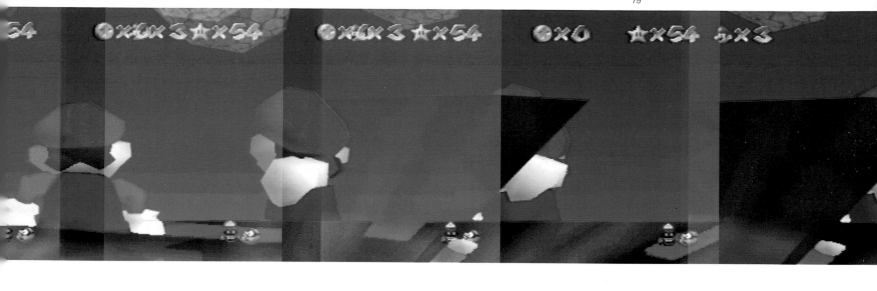

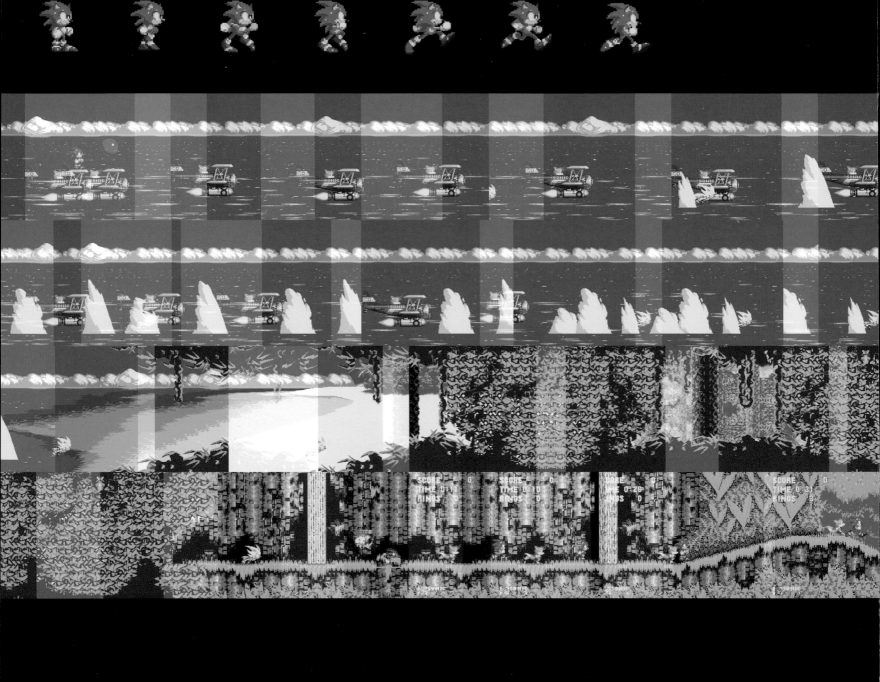

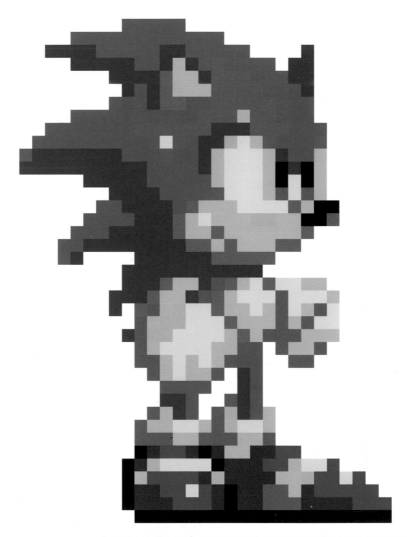

Sonic the Hedgehog. Sega's mascot I facing page: **sonic 3** I sega I genesis I 1994

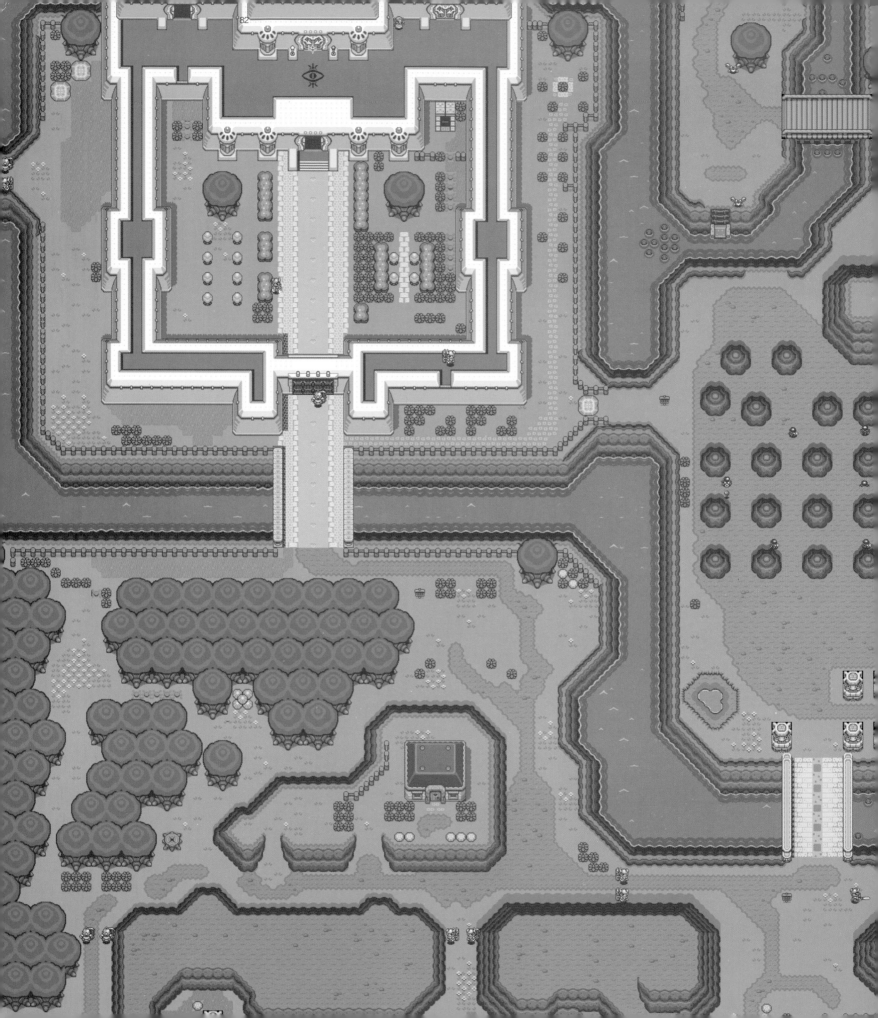

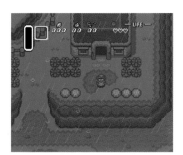

zelda 3 | nintendo | snes | 1992

myst | cyan | red orb | pc | 1993

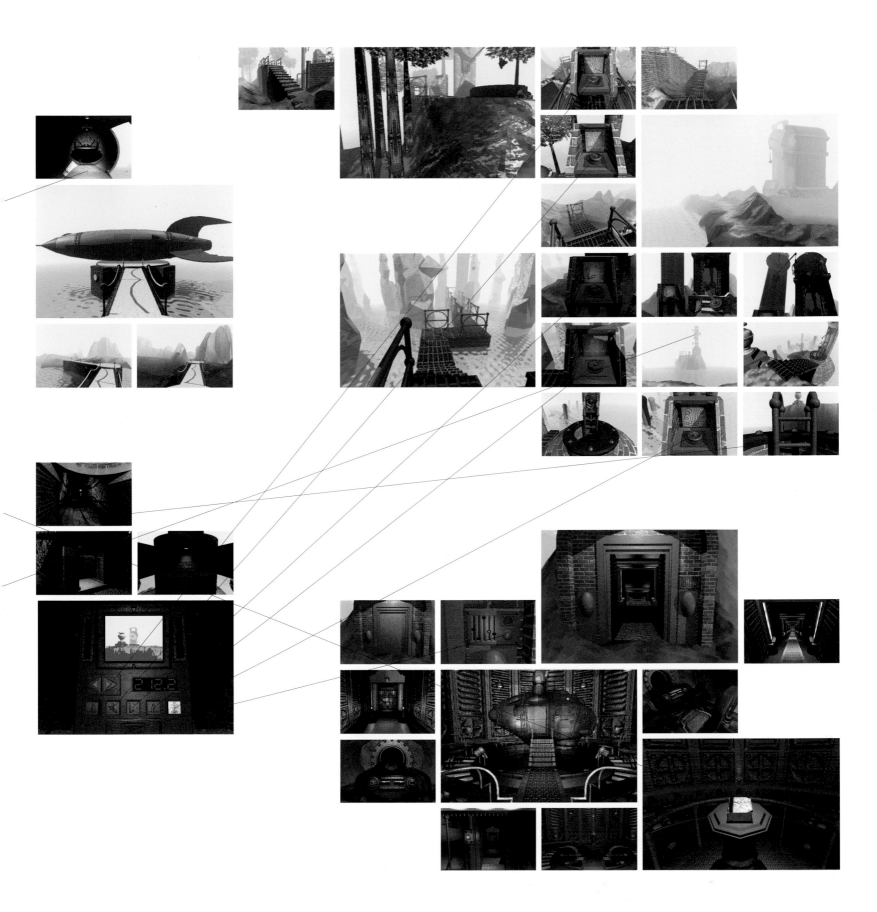

An Interview with **Robyn** and **Rand Miller**, the Creators of *Myst* and *Riven*

Brothers Robyn and Rand Miller led separate lives until 1987 when Rand, the eldest and the most technically-minded, had an idea for a children's game while he was working as a programmer at the Citizens' National Bank of Henderson. He called his artistic younger brother, Robyn, who at the time was studying anthropology at Washington University, to ask him if he would illustrate the game. Robyn took the narrative he was given and created an interactive environment. The collaboration between the brothers has now been going on for over ten years.

Their first game, *The Manhole*, won the Software Publishers Association award in 1988 for the best new use of a computer. *The Manhole* was a totally different interactive world, a non-threatening environment in which it was not possible to push the wrong button or get lost. After their first success, Robyn and Rand went on to make *Cosmic Osmo and the Worlds Beyond the Mackerel*. The Millers' objective this time was to create a world that both children and adults would enjoy. 'The time we spent working on the early children's projects was mostly a time of exploration and experimentation for us. We had stumbled across a new medium and we wanted to see what we could do with it,' says Robyn, 'but finally we were ready to meet the challenge of creating a world that appealed to grown-ups and we were ready to make the player the main character of an interactive story.' The brothers set to work on *Myst*. Released in September 1993, *Myst* provided a new experience for PC owners who wanted to play something different from arcade games. It is a considered and meditative game with no people and no violence, totally unlike anything that had come before it. The game starts on Myst Island; the player is given virtually no information, they merely understand that they need to work out what has happened. *Myst* has sold over 3.5 million copies and has stayed in the games charts for over four years, making it the most popular CD-Rom game of all time.

The follow-up, *Riven*, was a long time in coming. When it was finally released in late 1997 it filled five disks. *Riven* and *Myst* are the same kind of game in that they both have beautifully constructed, sparsely populated environments. Both games are navigated with the same point-click cursor interaction and both contain puzzles of a mechanical nature. *Riven* is a more immersive game than *Myst* as its wonderful sound and graphics draw the player into the game. Both games are about exploring and interacting with a mentally challenging environment. It will be interesting to see where the Miller brothers go from here.

What influences and inspirations led you to create these beautiful worlds?
Robyn: We've had a number of common influences among the three of us (I'm including Richard Vander Wende, who co-directed the project with me), most notably *Star Wars*. I was a kid when I first saw that movie, and I was astonished and transported. It was a place that I wanted to go to. The early Disney movies also had a tremendous influence on Richard and myself. Other personal influences include Dr Suess' children's books, *The Lord of the Rings* and the novels of Jules Verne. These are the types of influences that can be seen most clearly in *Myst* and *Riven*.

It could be said that *Myst* and *Riven* are more than computer games, they are works of art. They stand out. Why do you think so many games are stylistically similar?
Robyn: I feel that most games are dissimilar (rather than similar, as you say) to *Riven* and *Myst*. But that's one of the nice things about multimedia. With the advent of multimedia, not just one new medium has been introduced, but many. The content and style of products range from educational, to sports-styled games, to multi-player environments, to *Riven* and *Myst*. What Cyan has done represents just one minuscule segment of the entire range of styles and possibilities. It's kind of interesting right now. Everyone is in this stage of carving out their own little niche, and then figuring out how to make that niche work. It's actually a great time for media creators to get involved, because there are so many niches yet to be discovered. This is still a very infant medium. It's still very open to outsiders, to small groups, even to kids working out of their basements.
Rand: As far as our work being works of art, I don't think I would go that far. We have learned our particular craft well, but there's much more to being an artist than a craftsman. An artist (in my mind) expresses truth. He has mastered his craft so well that he can take it to the level of a deeper expression. I don't think we've done that yet.

Why do you think that people play games?
Robyn: For many different reasons, because there are many different types of games. A competitive game, like *Marathon*, is played as a game. Like a sport, it provides an outlet for stress and a means for competition. *Riven*, on the other hand, is a bit more story-based. It moves at a relaxed pace and is a bit more intellectually challenging. Perhaps it even stimulates an aesthetic sensibility. This doesn't make it better than a sport-like game, it just makes it different. Some people like movies, some people like watching (or participating in) sporting events, and some people like a little of both.

riven | cyan | red orb | pc | 1997

Rand: People play games for entertainment, so the larger question is 'Why do people want to be entertained?'. I believe the root for that desire is a need to explore and learn. Exploration and learning was part of life for early man. For the people who couldn't take part directly in the adventure, storytelling began – a way to 'bring the adventure home'. The best storytellers mastered their craft enough to tug deep within our emotions; they could hold our attention with a story while at the same time teaching us truth. For the people who couldn't experience the thrill of the hunt, there was entertainment, in the form of games, that would provide a bit of the same feeling. At the same time, useful skills were learned. Almost all of our forms of entertainment today seem to somehow come from that need to explore and learn.

Do you believe that the violence of some computer games has a destructive influence on society?

Robyn: Yes… absolutely. Violence, and any other type of content, always has an effect on people. In the case of a movie, like *Titanic*, violence is used to make the audience contemplate their own mortality, which is a good thing. In a game, like *Marathon*, the audience (or participant) begins to become comfortable with the concept that they have no mortality, nor do their opponents. Games like *Marathon* become nothing but more and more realistic. The low-res representation of a human will soon become something that is extremely realistic and believable. This should disturb us.

Rand: Violence is a tool. Lessons learned through violence are learned well, and not forgotten quickly. Storytellers have always known that. The problem comes from the fact that violence can be used gratuitously, when nothing is taught. When it's used only as a means to get attention, and nothing worthwhile is communicated, then violence becomes a dangerous tool.

How can you better what you have done already?

Robyn: *Myst* and *Riven* were environments. They were places. In terms of creating an interesting place, we have only scratched the surface of what can be done in this medium.

Rand: As I mentioned above, we can strive to add some value to our entertainment. We can try to add truth. We can also become better at our craft, exploring different ways to experience exploration.

What role does each brother have in the creation of a game?

Robyn: Rand was producer. Richard and I were co-directors.

What comes first when you prepare a game, the story or the graphic look?

Robyn: The story always comes first… or at least an outline of the story. The details of the story and the graphic look evolve together because they are so inextricably entwined.

What single thing do you think could improve the experience of gameplay?

Robyn: I'm not sure what you mean by gameplay, but what I think would improve *Riven* the most would be intelligent people inhabiting the place. If creatures had the ability to interact intelligently with the user, then the environment would be improved ten-fold. I don't mean some sort of stiff, pre-programmed interaction; I mean an intelligent and emotion-rich interaction.

Rand: There are so many ways to improve the experience, it all depends on what experience we want to improve. We can always make the environment more and more convincing, so that the exploration seems real. We can add characters, as Robyn mentioned, that make it more believable. We can add elements of competition or co-operation that add other experiences to the mix. I don't think that any one 'game' will be able to do everything, though.

In ten years' time what new experiences do you think games might be able to offer the player?

Robyn: Perhaps an improved interface, better story integration, better graphics, and smoother integration of characters. And probably a lot of other things that I've never even thought of.

Rand: See above!

What constitutes a good game?

Robyn: Good content. The technology is the vehicle for this content, but the content is so crucial. It's easy to be tempted by technology when you're making a game, because you're so surrounded with it. But the content must remain the focus. You see this mistake made all the time in movies, where the easy answer is often, 'let's add more effects', rather than, 'let's fix the story'. The games that are successful – the games that people like (even if they are violent) – are those that have some attempt at content.

Rand: I think it's all storytelling. Most people have very few adventures any more. Or if they do, they're mostly limited to vacations in safe locations or theme parks. What they seek is something that gives them a feeling of exploring, whether it's told to them on a movie screen, or given to them as a 'world' on an interactive device. But it's the story that makes it good. Either the one they're told, or the one they experience. If there is some element of truth that can be conveyed at the same time, then it also makes it worthwhile.

riven | cyan | red orb | pc | 1997

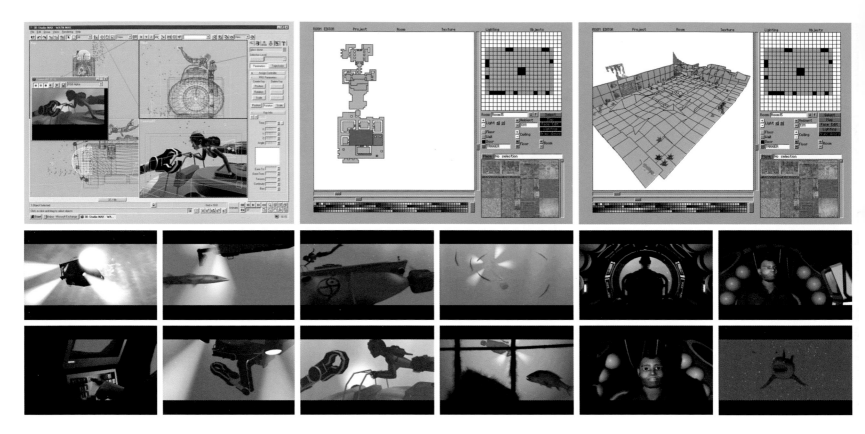

tomb raider **1/2** | core | eidos | pc + playstation | 1996/7

An Interview with **Toby Gard**, the Creator of **Lara Croft** and *Tomb Raider*

It is hard to believe that Lara Croft emerged from the mind of Toby Gard in 1994. What is more astounding is that at the time he was only 21 years old. Gard had always been fascinated by animation; it was a hobby that became a career. After an art foundation course he was unemployed for months and would spend hours on his home computer making animations. He finally sent some examples of his work to Core Design, who hired him. When he first started work his role was simply to put forward ideas for games, then he was put to work on one of Core's titles, a job he hated so much he refuses to speak much about it or even to name the game.

After only a year and a half in the business he hit upon the idea for *Tomb Raider*. 'The initial idea was for the game and not the character,' says Gard, 'the main character wasn't even going to be female at the start. The concept was instead to have a character which could be controlled in a 3D environment in a game which was created in a filmic way. At the time *Virtua Fighter 2* had just been released. I wanted to combine those characters with enjoyable adventuring. Then we had the idea to make the game the reverse of everything that had come before. Not only is there a heroine instead of a hero, she is also English and all the "baddies" are foreigners. It is not that I am a xenophobe, I was just playing with a stereotype. The English are normally cast as the "baddies".'

So what is Lara's story? She was born with a silver spoon in her mouth, the daughter of Lord and Lady Henshingly Croft, no less. She was tragically separated from her parents in an air crash over the Himalayas in which they were killed instantly. Poor Lara had to throw aside her upper-crust upbringing and learn some survival skills. Once down from the mountain she spent the next few years learning about ancient artefacts – enough in fact to become the female equivalent of Indiana Jones and thus stage the first great epic of her life, *Tomb Raider*.

Before devising Lara's final look – brown hot-pants and a green vest – Gard toyed with many different possibilities, including a military look and very baggy trousers. 'First she was a large amount of *Tank Girl*, then she looked like Neneh Cherry, finally she became a female version of Indiana Jones.' In all it took nearly four months until Gard was happy with her. The end result is an empowered woman; not a sex object in a smutty way, but an inaccessible, gun-toting bitch. 'I don't think Lara was designed as a sex object, she wasn't meant to be tarty, she had to be self-dependent. The most important thing to me was that she shouldn't ever be in a love-interest situation. That is why I also chose to make her upper class – it makes her even more untouchable.'

Gard chuckles at the mention of her ample breasts. It is widely acknowledged that these were created by accident, but this, says Gard, came out of a silly remark made in an interview with a journalist. The story of a happy accident is unfounded – her chest was entirely intentional.

Even though it took two years to bring Lara to life, *Tomb Raider* was a fantastic investment. The team at Core was young, and there were only six people working on the project. Gard estimates that the game was made for around £500,000, very cheap for a blockbuster. Creating it was a pain-staking

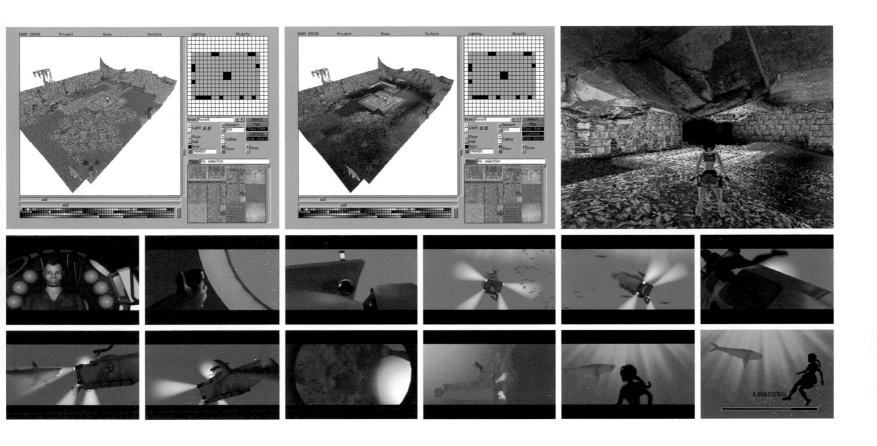

process. After producing sketches, the designers had to build the characters in a 3D package. Then there was the tricky bit, the animation; Gard says that Lara's standard running and moving about alone incorporates around 5,000 frames of animation. This does not include the extensive animation sequences that run between the levels and at the start and the finish of the game. There are fifteen levels in *Tomb Raider* and some of the sequences contain over 2,000 frames of animation each.

So why aren't there more intelligent heroines gracing our screens? 'It would be useful,' says Gard, 'if more women designed games. I really do think it is a question of attitude. If more women designed games we would get away from testosterone-led gameplay. Most of the women in games before Lara wore thigh-high boots and thongs. At the time we created *Tomb Raider* I don't think there had ever been a good game with a heroine.'

Lara's popularity can also be linked to the fact that at the time of *Tomb Raider*'s release in 1996 the UK was in the grip of 'girl power', spurred on by the larger-than-life British pop band the Spice Girls. Lara has generated more column inches than many wannabe actors and pop stars. She has been talked about in nearly every newspaper and magazine in the UK. It can safely be said that Eidos, the game's publisher, went to town on the marketing. 'People are always using sexy women to sell unsexy products,' says Gard, 'so when the product is actually a sexy woman you can go mad.' However, Eidos and Core are now in a position where they must tread carefully; if you are going to create hype you have to be able to live up to it, and with two games rumoured to be in the pipeline, content must evolve.

Toby Gard is not concerned with how *Tomb Raider* progresses – he did not work on *Tomb Raider II* or even get a credit on the packaging; 'I got so tired of it all', he says. Offers to work for other developers came flooding in, but instead of going to someone else, Gard set up his own company, Confounding Factor, helped with an advance for his new title from Interplay. Based in the south-west of England, Confounding Factor will release their debut title *Leviathan* at the end of 1999. Gard says that *Leviathan* is far more advanced than *Tomb Raider*, involving much more animation plus the added bonus of having several characters to choose from. Putting it together is proving to be a pain-staking task: 'The complexity of games is increasing. If you look at games today compared to the Spectrum, we are getting into very complex simulations of life and events. Nowadays there is much more work in a game than there is in a film; this is because we have to cover all the possibilities.'

Despite *Tomb Raider*'s phenomenal success, Gard modestly rejects the idea that it was a ground-breaking game. '*Tomb Raider* was a logical progression for games; it just happened that people focused in on the character. The thing is, you can't just have a good character, you have to have a good game to go with it, and *Tomb Raider* is a good game.'

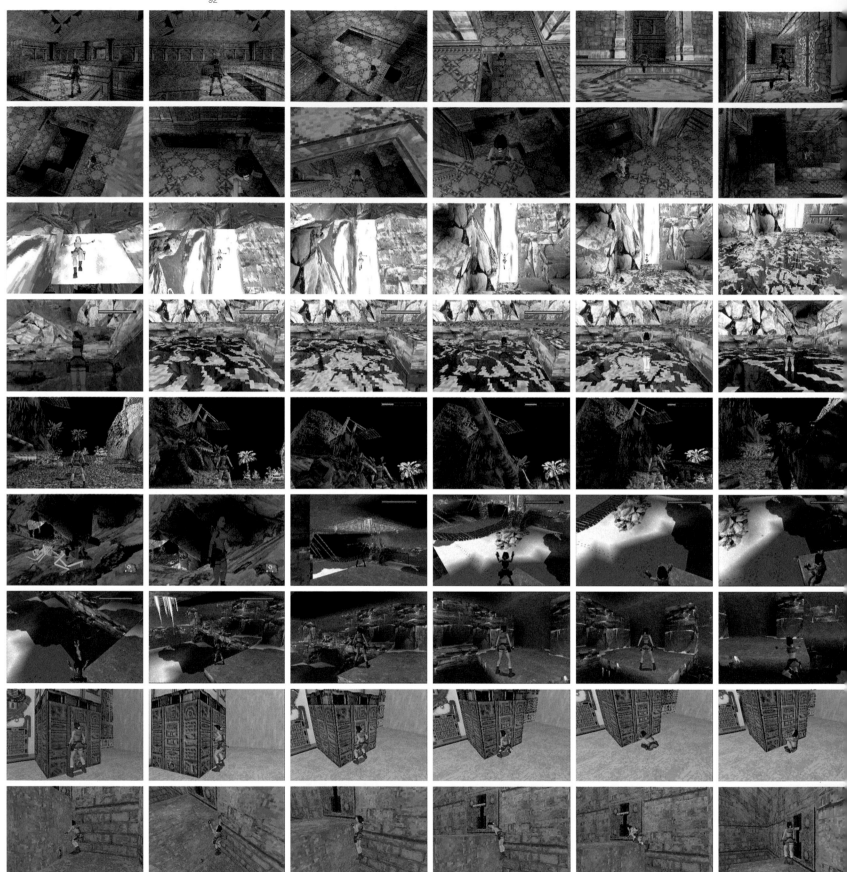

tomb raider 1/2 | core | eidos | pc/playstation | 1996–7

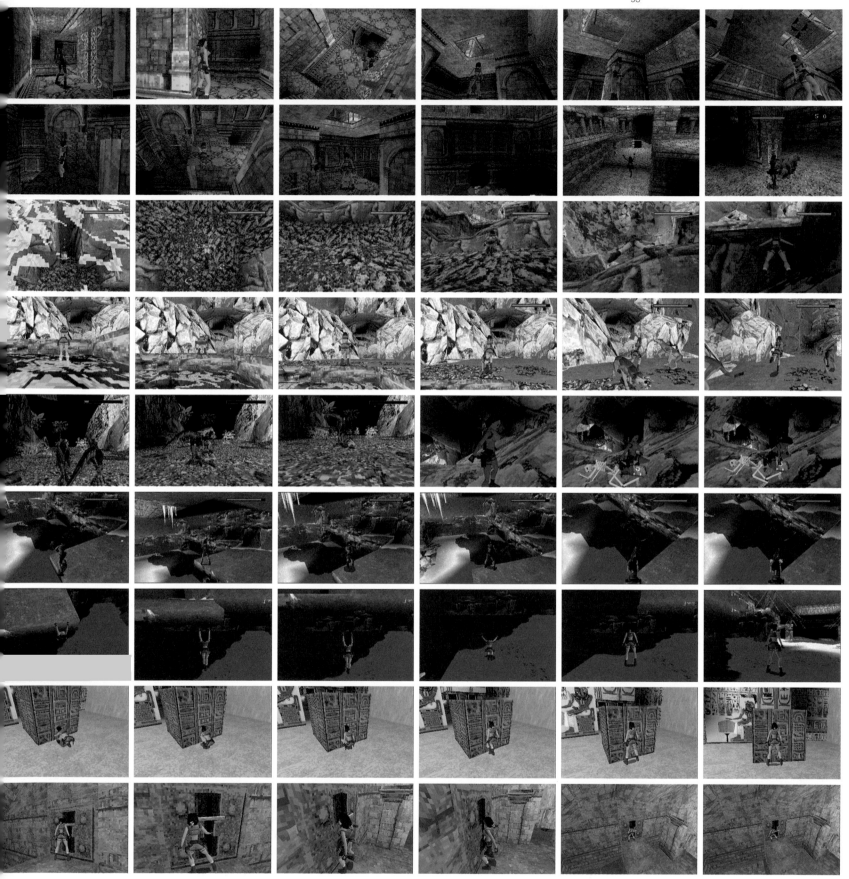

crash bandicoot 2 | naughty dog | sony | playstation | 1997

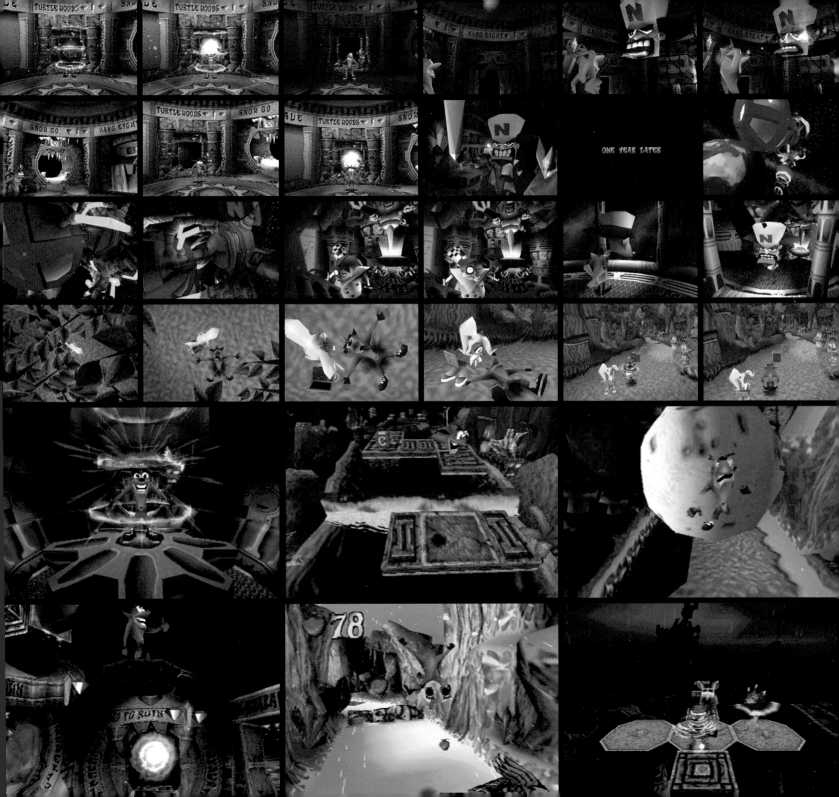

crash bandicoot 2 | naughty dog | sony | playstation | 1997

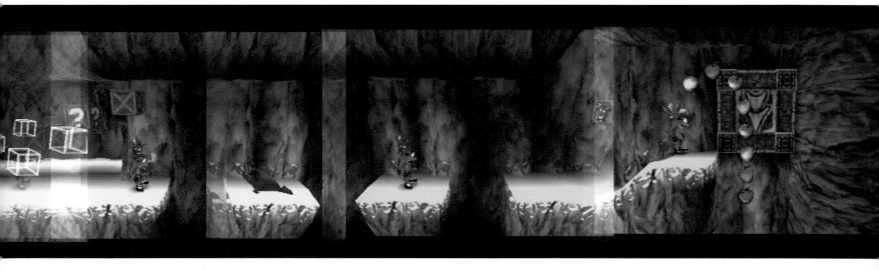

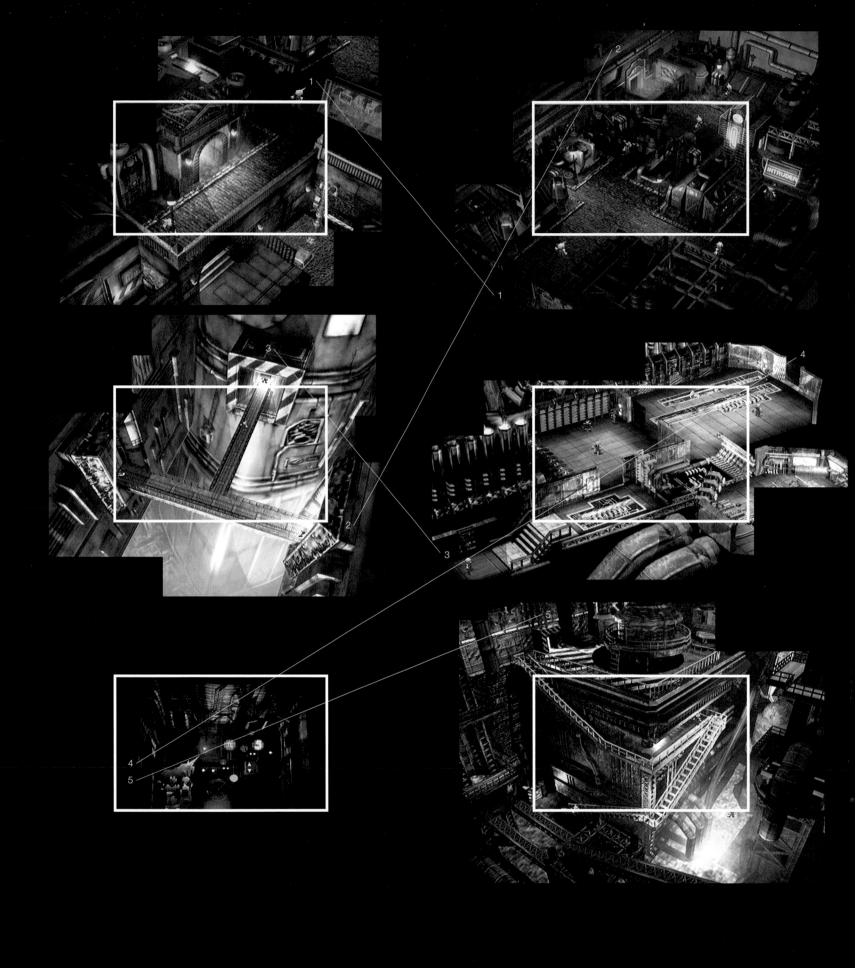

final fantasy vii | squaresoft | eidos | playstation | 1997

bladerunner | westwood studios | virgin interactive | pc | 1997

Animation and Film Sequences

Animation and film sequences have been a tradition within games ever since *Pac-Man* chased Pinky *et al* at the end of every level. From rather humble beginnings these sequences have developed into extravaganzas which consume around a third of a game's budget. While some people complain that they are a waste of money, film and animation sequences are necessary because without them it is incredibly difficult to convey a plot. The sequences are a vehicle for supplying complex information that is relevant to the game, while also serving to immerse the player in the story. They provide the purpose for the gameplay. How they look is very varied.

On loading up a brand new purchase it is standard practice to meet games' characters via a movie. The 'goodies' and the 'baddies' are introduced, and the player learns who has done what to whom. The opening sequences provide the player with their objectives. At the end of every level it is customary to have another film which both acts as a reward for completing the level and advances the plot. Nowadays it is unacceptable not to have a spectacular film – a grand finale – at the end of a game. In the past, film and animation sequences were very much bolted on to the games, offering little to

enhance the actual gameplay. Unfortunately for players it was often the case that the better the film the worse the game as developers used movies to make up for poor play. The Bitmap Brothers' game *Z* is an example of this. For years, long-suffering players paid to be subjected to a kind of virtual *Falcon Crest*: an unknown actor standing in front of a blue screen, with no art direction and sets that looked home-made. The fact that games companies often produce all the film sequences in house may serve as some kind of an explanation but not an excuse.

A few games developers have taken the step of employing recognized talent. Electronic Arts' *Wing Commander IV* starred Mark Hamill (alias Luke Skywalker); it became more of a movie than a game. In another Electronic Arts extravaganza for their interactive movie game, *The Darkening*, Christopher Walken and John Hurt, actors who would not normally be classed in the same profession as *Crash Bandicoot*, were filmed on set at Pinewood Studios, England. The game had a budget of $6.5 million.

resident evil 2 | capcom | virgin interactive | playstation | 1998

Although it was a graphic triumph, the gameplay was not very impressive. The moral of the story being that graphics can impress but gameplay always rules.

More recently, Westwood Studios threw caution to the wind with their version of the seminal science-fiction movie *Blade Runner*. Considering *Blade Runner*'s cult following and rich graphic history, the game's producers had a real chance of creating something great. The game opens with full-screen, 16-bit colour cinematics. All the characters and sets have been rendered using motion capture. Despite this the game still remains unconvincing, probably due to the poor acting and the ill-fitting voice-overs. It is really hard to be atmospheric on screen – unless you use animation.

Since the cost of the equipment used for 3D rendering has fallen, animation has been used within games like never before. Animation is no longer simply bolted on to either side of a level, it appears within the games, for example, in character celebrations in sports or fighting games. Perhaps the most successful and imaginative use of animation can be seen in Squaresoft's *Final Fantasy VII*. The animation here is not only astounding but has been seamlessly integrated into the game. One minute the player is in complete control of their character, and the next they are being transported into a fully animated environment. The best thing and a first for the industry is that these animations do not require any load time. This can be expected to become the norm.

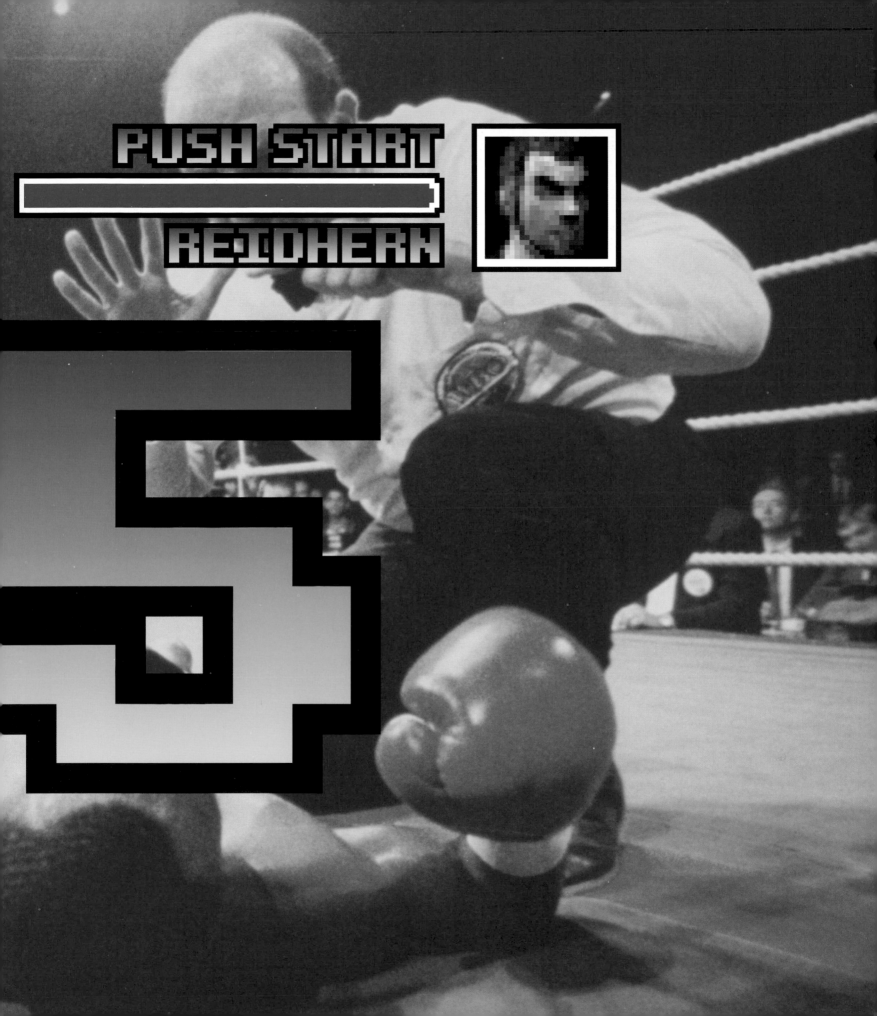

fight

Beat-em-ups are the most popular arcade games. They provide players with the chance to be a super-hero. They are games in which a player's personal skill, dexterity and knowledge of the game will give them the upper hand against their opponent.

Nowadays these games follow a certain formula. There is a selection of Mangaesque characters to choose from, each of which has different skills, 'special moves' and characteristics. The player must learn about the characters: which one has speed, who has power and who has technique. It is the norm that these characters each have their own story and their own reason to fight in the arena. As the games are sold worldwide, the characters possess a mixture of global characteristics, from the American hunk, muscle bound and blonde to the Japanese Manga vixen.

Capcom released the first 3D simulation fighting game, *Street Fighter*, in 1987. However, at this time the technology was not developed enough to provide the really fast moves demanded by joystick action. The characters would not do what you wanted. Capcom's second version, *Street Fighter II*, arrived in 1991. At its launch it was probably the best computer game ever released. Capcom's designers had developed a clever joystick and button-scanning program that revolutionized their game. This could quickly sense and react to the different motions of the player. The game could be played in two modes: arcade, where the player could progress through different levels fighting, or one-to-one combat, involving a choice of eight characters, a format present in today's fighting games.

The race was on to produce the best game. Following Capcom's lead was Midway's *Mortal Kombat*. Released in 1992, *Mortal Kombat* helped to redefine the genre. This game was blood-thirsty: players could disembowel their opponent to 'finish' him or perhaps rip his head off or pull his heart out. The result of this was predictable: both the press and politicians accused the game of morally corrupting young people. Of course, there is nothing youth likes more than a spot of moral corruption, and the

In the meantime, Capcom, riding high on a multi-million dollar wave, had been bringing out numerous different versions of *Street Fighter II* – prequels, sequels and even a film, most of which bombed. Then in 1995 Sega brought out *Virtua Fighter 2*. This was the first fighting game to have 3D polygon char-acters, and its smooth, clean graphics with realistically human movement made all the difference. The characters could perform spectacular 360-degree spins before kicking their opponents squarely in the jaw. To play well required skill.

Today all fighting games use this technology. The most impressive beat-em-up to date has been Sony's *Tekken* series. *Tekken*'s super characters wipe out the competition with their pace, aggression and clothing. The characters' moves are created using motion capture (see introduction to Win); the moves of real martial arts masters were gathered and added to the game for realism. The long-awaited *Tekken 3* adds a panda bear to the series' already impressive range of characters.

As we enter the Age of Aquarius, beat-em-ups are even going back to their spiritual origins. To play Sony's *Bushido Blade* you have to incorporate both the stance and philosophy of the Bushido warrior. Players have got so used to the hyper pace of the genre, however, that spiritual alternatives are unlike-ly to take off.

tekken 3 | namco | playstation | 1998

01-06 international karate plus | c64 | 1987 | 07-08 pro wrestling | nintendo | nes | 1986 | 09-12 way of the exploding fist | melbourne house | spectrum | 1985 | 13-14 yie ar kung fu | konami | msx | 1985 | 15-24 yu yu hakusho tokubetuhen | namco | snes | 1994 | 25-28 altered beast | sega | pc engine | 1988 | 29-30 kung-fu master | data east | arcade | 1985 | 31-42 art of fighting | snk | kac | snes | 1993 | 43-45 evander holyfield's reel deal boxing | acme interactive | sega | snes | 1992 | 46-48 yie ar kung fu | konami | arcade | 1985 | 49-50 karateka | jordan mechner | broderbund | c64 | 1984 | 51-52 wrestle-mania | acclaim | nes | 1988 | 53-54 wrestlemania steel cage | ljn | sculptured software inc. | nes | 1992 | 55-72 street fighter ii turbo | capcom | snes | 1993

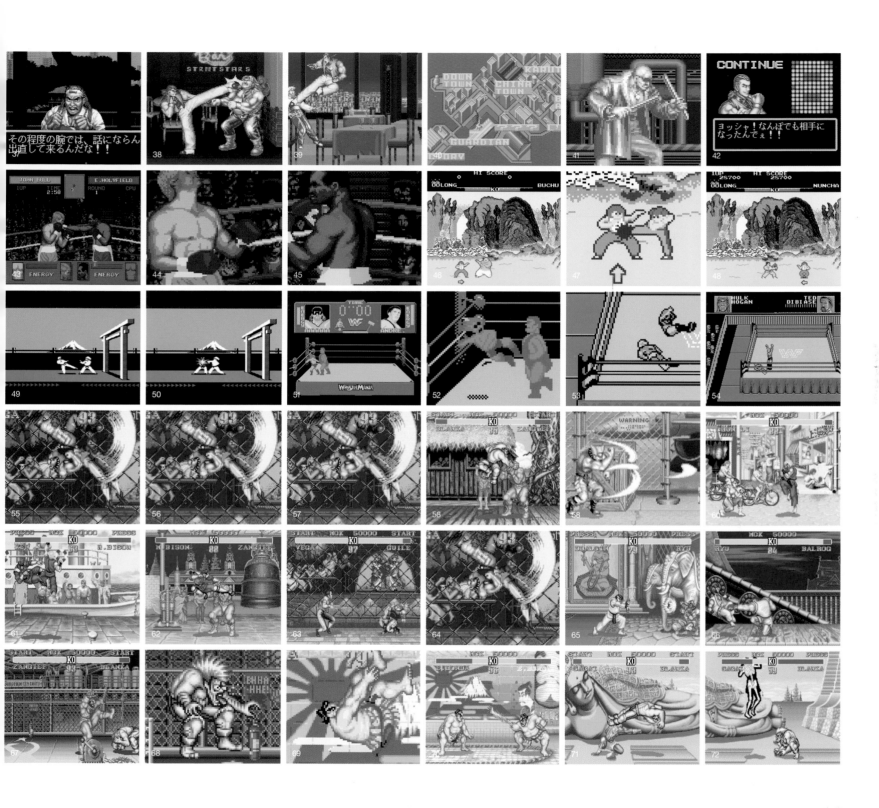

way of the exploding fist | melbourne house | zx spectrum | 1985

SINDEL JADE

01-10 **soul blade** 01 hwang 02 rock 03 taki 04 sophitia 05 mitsurugi 06 siegfried 07 seung mina 08 li long 09 voldo 10 cervantes | **11-20 fighter's destiny** 11 abdul 12 bob 13 boro 14 leon 15 meiling 16 ninja 17 pierre 18 ryuji 19 tomahawk 20 valerie | **21-30 virtua fighter** 21 lion rafale 22 pai chan 23 akira yuki 24 shun di 25 jacky bryant 26 sarah bryant 27 kage maru 28 jeffrey mcwild 29 wolf hawkfield 30 lau chan | **31-40 street fighter ii turbo** 31 ryu 32 dhalism 33 sagat 34 ken 35 m. bison 36 chun li 37 zangeif 38 e. honda 39 blanka 40 guile | **41-50 mortal kombat iv** 41 fujin 42 jarek 43 jax 44 johnny cage 45 kai 46 liu kang 47 quan chi 48 reiko 49 reptile 50 scorpion | facing page: **ultimate mortal kombat** | avalanche | sculptured software | williams | midway | snes | 1996

virtua fighter | sega | saturn | 1997

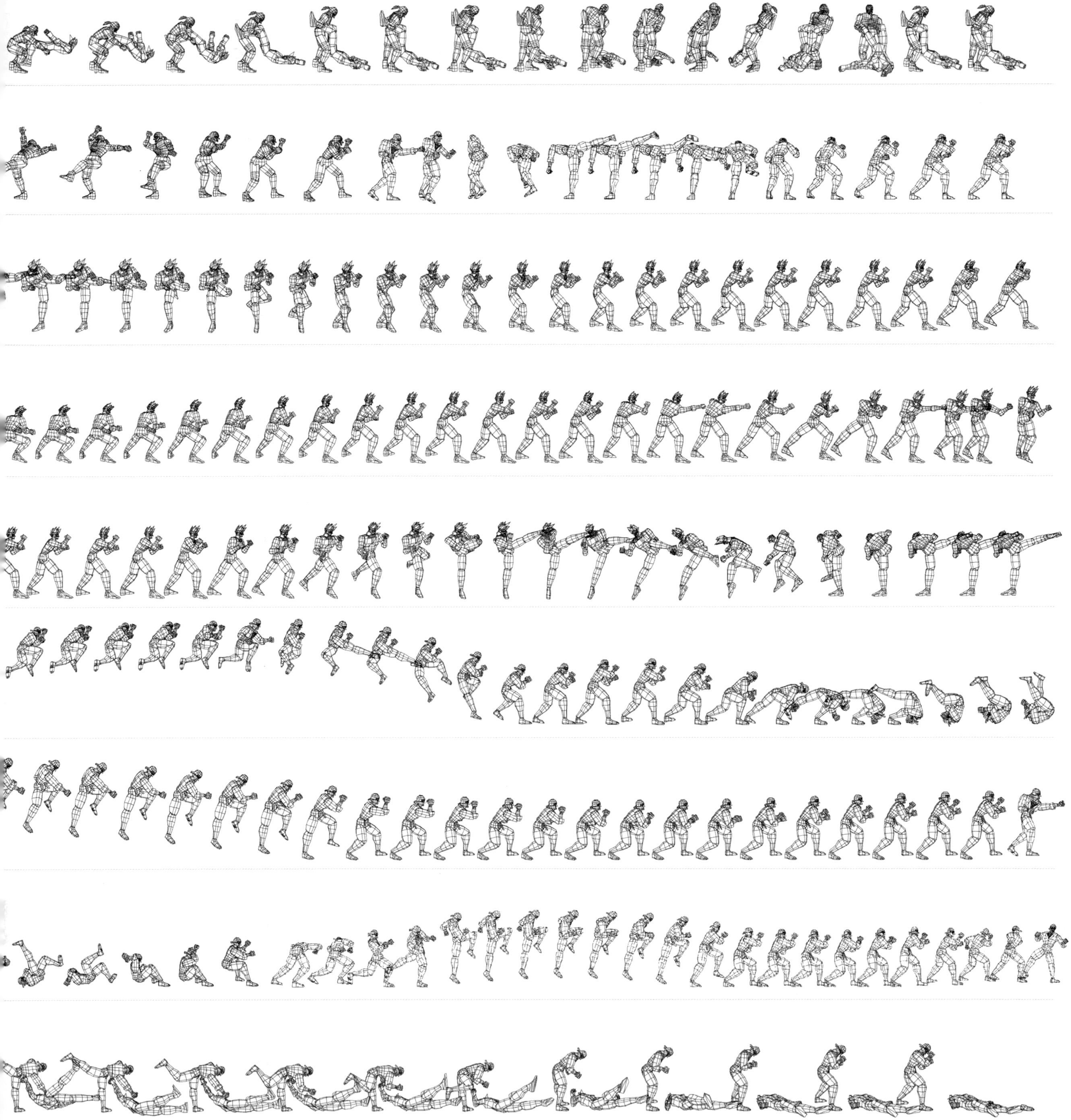

virtua fighter | sega | saturn | 1997

116

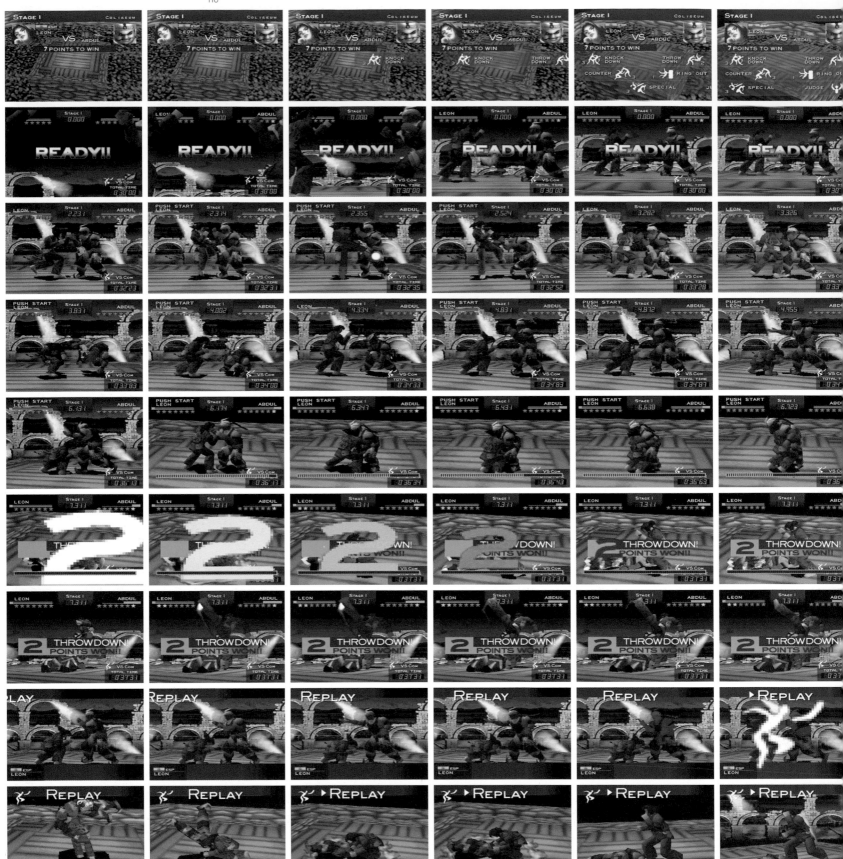

fighter's destiny | ocean | genki | imagineer | n64 | 1998

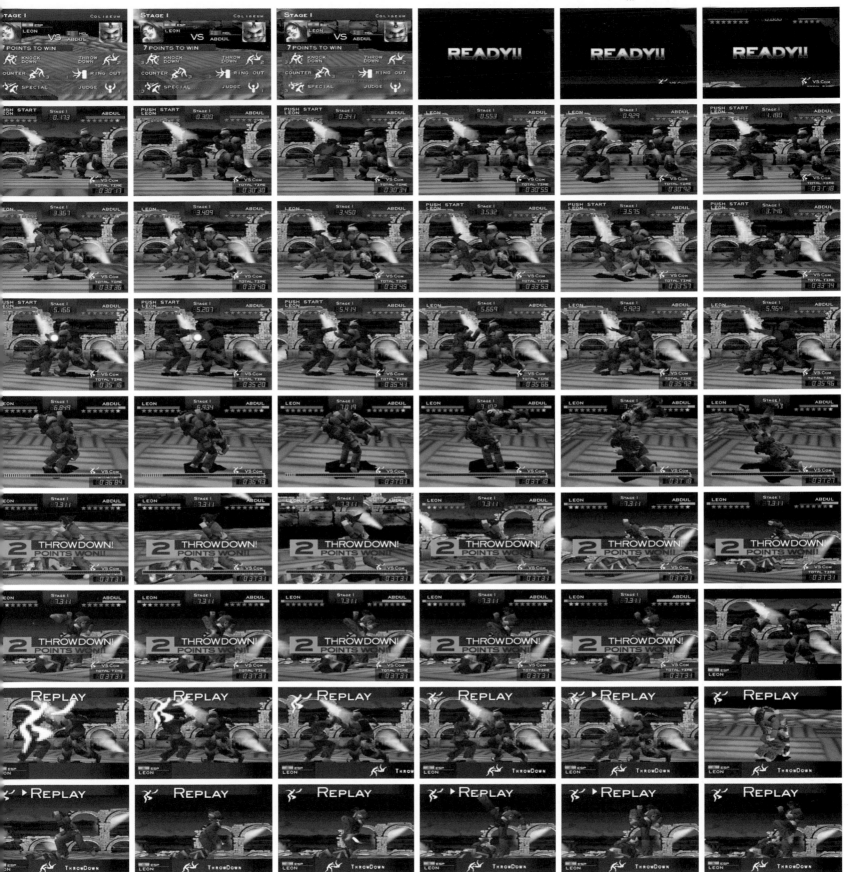

control

Strategy games fall roughly into two categories: god games, where you control a world, and war games where you take over a world. These games provide a different experience for the player from that offered by character-driven games. Strategy games are more about brain-teasing, plotting and planning than mind-blowing effects. Although the graphics do not stand comparison with those of games such as *Tekken*, however, they have a charm of their own, and *Myth* and *Dungeon Keeper* are evidence that they are improving.

War games have been around for decades. In the 1970s, paper-based war games sold in booklets were very popular; they also manifested themselves in other more familiar family games such as *Risk*. The computer-based games currently enjoy a diverse following of all age groups. The rise in PC sales has been responsible for the boom in this genre. The situations posed by the games are real: the player is not blasting aliens in a far outpost of the universe but using their brainpower to resolve earthly conflicts. Mainstream games such as *Tomb Raider* are only now beginning to put the player in a situation that approximates to real life. These games demand sophisticated planning and tactics; a goal must be set and adhered to.

In 1989 a British company called Bullfrog released *Populous*, the genre-defining god game. *Populous* was the first game to cast the player as god. Rather than being a character, the player ruled the world from above, levelling the land, manipulating nature itself and persuading the inhabitants to follow them. By 1990 Bullfrog had sold over a million copies of the game; nearly ten years later *Populous: The Third Coming* is due for release and boasts a more powerful AI engine than any god game to date.

Another legendary series of god games is Maxis' *SimCity*. *SimCity* was created for the 16-bit consoles and was released in the same year as *Populous*. It charges the player with the task of building a city, first arranging the power, water and the roads in a logical and working fashion, then deciding where to place the schools and other buildings. If the player runs the city like a madman, their people will revolt. Bullfrog and Maxis initially had trouble finding a publisher for their games as no one wanted to take a gamble with a new genre. Eventually US publisher Electronic Arts took up the cause, and it now owns both companies.

Strategy/god games such as *Ultima* and *Myth* have recently had a large uptake online. The games work well in an online network as there are no complicated graphics to download. The publisher of *Ultima* is using a *Doom*-like marketing offensive to reach their audience, distributing the games on CD-Roms that can be networked on the internet, and building up a thriving online community.

The internet seems to offer a huge market for strategy games since they do not require excellent graphics to make them successful. With the hardware and software now available, however, a graphic revolution is almost certain to take place in these games, and the danger is that this will be at the expense of the gameplay. The race is on to attract consumers, and developers are increasingly placing the look of a game above its content.

simcity 2000 | maxis | pc + macintosh | 1995

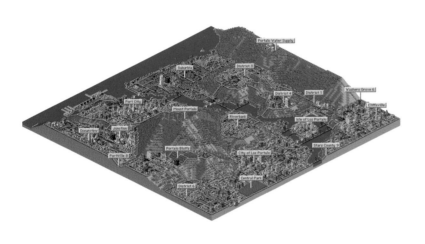

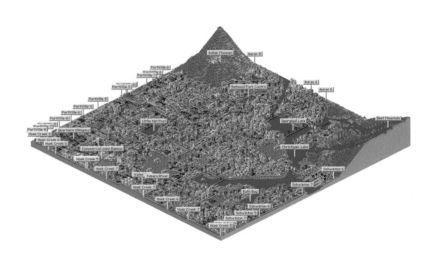

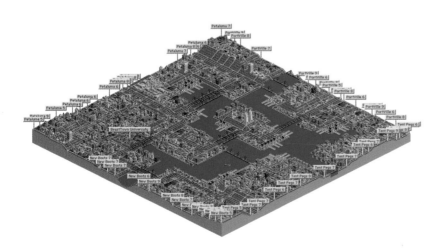

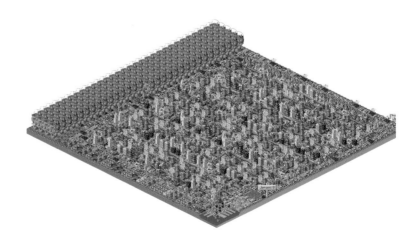

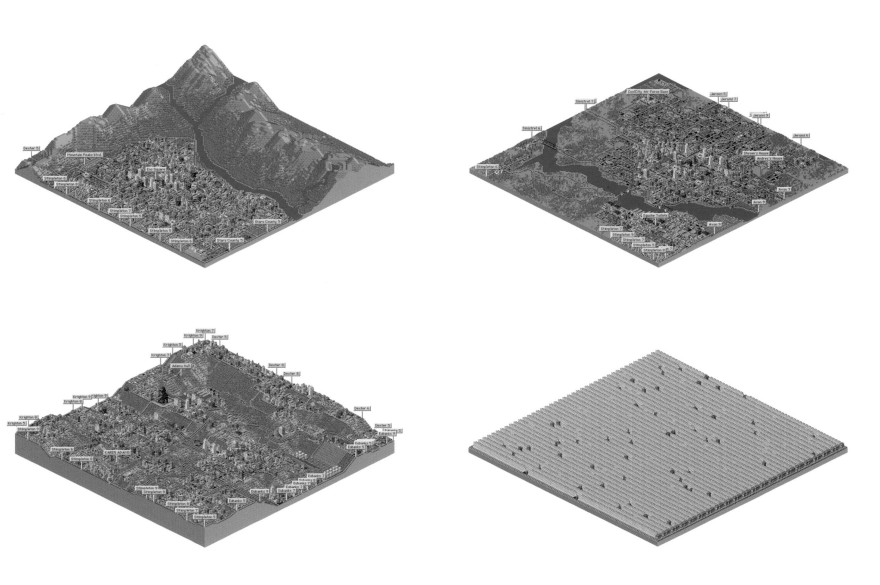

 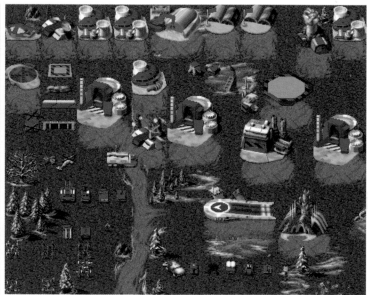

command and conquer | westwood studios | virgin interactive | macintosh | 1995

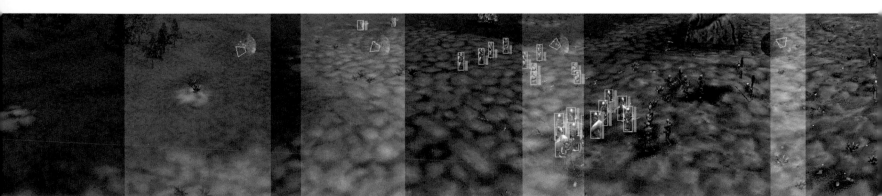

myth: the fallen lords | bungie | sybex inc. | macintosh | 1997

← Check in Zones C to G

Airport Information
Left Baggage

↑ Underground
Trains
Buses
Terminals 1 & 2

fly

The flight simulation community is a very demanding group to develop games for as they are perfectionists, obsessed with experiencing maximum realism from the games they play. The games normally take the form of first-person simulations. The aim of a simulation game is to give the player a taste of what controlling complex equipment such as a plane is like, in an environment that responds in a similar way to the real world. The player can feel some of the thrill of putting an aircraft into a tail spin without experiencing any of the danger. The situations being enacted can have many scenarios, and each game varies in realism, for example, you could be flying over the Baltic on a mission or travelling between two fictional planets.

The really addictive pull of a great simulation game is that it provides the player with the cognitive and physical elements of doing the real thing. The joy of these interactive microcosms is that the user may experiment in them and quickly see the effect of a move; a simulation game should provide the player with authentic feedback about their errors.

The rules of flight simulation games often include mission objectives which, particularly in a multi-player environment, introduce an element of competition and determine the winner. Commanding a squadron certainly has more appeal than flying around alone. The skills the player acquires during the game is an education in its own right. Indeed, the armed forces and airline companies have been using advanced simulations for years to train their staff. It is rumoured that the multi-million dollar software used to develop these advanced simulations for training is then watered down and repackaged for games developers.

However realistic a flight simulation may be, the inner workings of a game are a poor substitute for the real thing. The object of a simulation game is to fool the user into believing that they are achieving something based on their own expectations of how the object that they are controlling works. Home entertainment is in fact a long way from actually achieving anything truly real. The main reason for this is the outdated methods of data input. Fans of flight sims are confined to playing on their PC, and the keyboard is a very poor substitute for the controls of a complex aircraft. Even though it is possible to custom program the keys, it is still a challenge to remember which is which. These games are so complicated that they could never be learnt in an arcade (see pages 140-1).

f-22 air dominance fighter | digital image design | ocean | pc | 1997

f/a 18 korea | graphic simulations | macintosh | 1992

f/a 18 hornet 3.0 | graphic simulations | macintosh | 1992

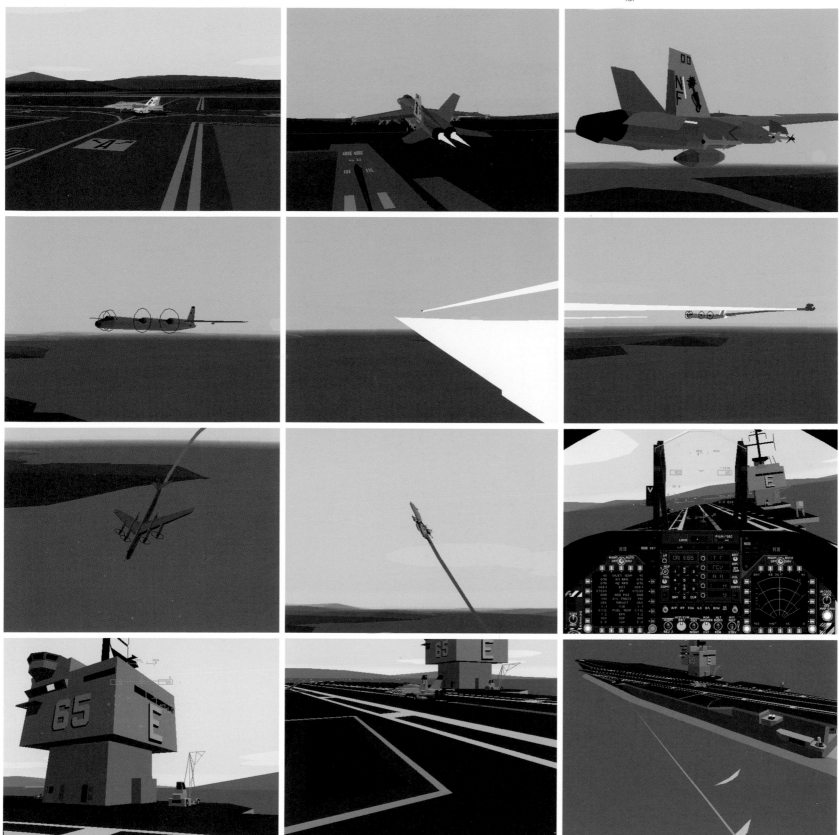

f/a **18** korea | graphic simulations | macintosh | 1992

f-22 air dominance fighter l digital image design l ocean l pc l 1997

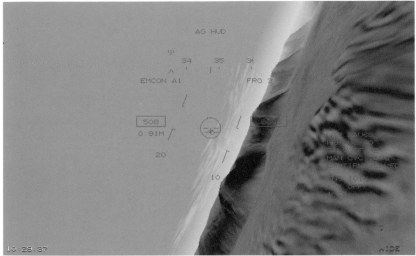

Digital Image Design: The Propeller Heads

In the north of England a company called Digital Image Design is producing flight simulations that are so realistic, the RAF use them for training. Although it is not unusual for simulators to be used by the armed forces, this is an achievement because the code used was written for games. Normally it is technology the military has produced that gets packaged for the mass markets (having spent millions on it they need to claw back some of the costs).

Martin Kenwright founded DID 'out of anger' in 1989. 'I was pissed off with my job earning £100 a week working on big games. My first game *F29 Retaliator* was made in my bedroom. The first publisher we took it to bought it.' Kenwright sold 300,000 copies of his game and occupied the number one spot for ten weeks. Since then DID has doubled in size every year.

'We haven't been profit-organized; we are not businessmen, yet we are the world leaders in our market which is US dominated. The key to a game's success is balance. We do better 3D graphics than our competitors. Now the sim genre is getting big we are looking at other markets.'

F-22 ADF is the twelfth flight sim DID has produced. The company has written around two-thirds of all European sims and will launch six titles in the next two years.

'Flight sim is a discrete genre,' says DID's project manager Don Whiteford. 'Ours is a hobbyist market. Customers are very fussy about what they want.' As a result DID try to make their games as realistic as possible. Their links with the RAF have had an undeniable benefit on their games.

'The project with the RAF started with our game *EF2000*,' says Whiteford. 'I was trying to glean how you drop bombs. How high you have to be, that sort of thing. At the time the RAF were fitting a laser device to guide bombs. They proposed that we made a PC simulator for them before they went ahead and fitted it.' Due to the relatively low cost of PCs the RAF could buy more of these units and they were happy with what they got. The bottom line is that PC graphics are good enough to use in military training.

To increase realism DID is looking to get satellite data for terrain mapping within their games. Some of this data is sold publicly and some is available from the army. Provided that DID can obtain all the terrain data from around the world (and it looks as though they might), they will be able to generate exact landscapes of the world. Their concept in a nutshell is a fully electronic global battlefield. Within the world the user would be able to fly any craft, drive any vehicle in the game and even be a soldier on the ground. DID's ground-based war game *Tank* works along these lines.

Until a real map can be generated DID has to make do with building its own virtual worlds. *F22 ADF*'s world took up an amazing four million square kilometres. Such a large space is necessary because a flight sim will not be convincing if you can see the edge of the world. In *F22 ADF* there are 1,500 planes all doing separate missions. These missions have very detailed objectives which lead to a mind-bending fourteen million permutations of the game. This makes platform programming seem easy. In platform games everything is pre-scripted; in other words if you walk past something, X will jump out at you. *F22* differs because there is an intelligent agent in the game that recommends and changes strategy as a real commander would, making decisions based on a player's skills, the weather, and so on. Added to this you can get a camera angle anywhere in the game. 'Now we really need TV directors to help us orchestrate these games. These camera views are realtime movies. They are camera views on a real and evolving virtual world,' says Whiteford.

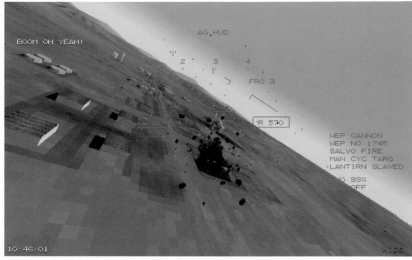

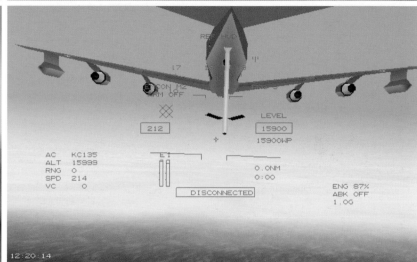

f-22 air dominance fighter 97 | digital image design | ocean | pc | 1997

The new PC-accelerated graphics cards allow DID the processing power to create all of this. Special effects such as mist, cloud, rain and snow are now easily produced, allowing spare power to go on programming AI. With the new engine 3D Dream, DID will ensure that every player's clock is connected to the game so that they can fly realtime day and night missions. What is more, DID already has a link with the US weather centre, the intention being to let the gamer/wing commander enact battles in current weather conditions anywhere in the world.

All the planes in the games produced by DID since *Euro Fighter* were created by an aeronautical engineer. He got hold of the files that gave the exact performance of the aircraft, took the shape and the data and then reverse-engineered it before putting in new controls. All the planes have six degrees of freedom of movement instead of the normal three. This gives the kind of realism that would be standard on any military sim.

There are many other elements that go into making a flight sim realistic. Different joysticks and controllers give the user the kind of resistance a pilot might feel on their controls. Sensors also provide shakes and kick-backs from the gun. Other subliminal cues help player immersion such as music. 'People get a lot of cues from sound. Before a battle the tempo of the music will increase. We would like to do things so that the other voices in the game will get higher before a battle,' says Whiteford. 'In a real battle if you were being attacked from behind you would hear the sound behind you and react. Special cues come from where an object is in 3D space. This is something that the army are also playing with. It would be interesting to create a game that has no visuals, only audio.'

The real revolution in the flight sim market will come with voice control. This will cut down on the horrendous key configurations each game requires. Voice control would also replace typing messages to people. VR headsets are promising but not really good enough as they can make a player feel sick and prevent them from seeing the keys that operate the rest of the game.

As far as future development for the industry is concerned, the emphasis is to create systems that allow a lot of creative control without needing intense coding or design. Whiteford would like to see the teams that work on games get smaller. 'Things like our world database will help that. You can set a game in North Korea or anywhere. We will be able to do an awful lot more with fewer people. At the moment we have teams of around 30 people for each game. We should bring it back to around eight, which is how the industry began.'

Chris Orton, also a co-founder, heads up the research and development areas. His job is to shape the future. 'The engine that we used for the game *ADF* has evolved over a number of years. However, it is a product that has reached its peak in *ADF*. There is a good chance that our next games will start with a clean sheet. In a lot of games there are visual imperfections every five minutes or so. The reason why they are not corrected is because the game is faster with these – without them it may not run at all. However, if we can render with 3D Studio now we should be able to achieve moving through a realistic environment in realtime in the next couple of years. I work by looking at workstations like Silicon Graphics. If I can make that happen on a PC, I'm not going far wrong.'

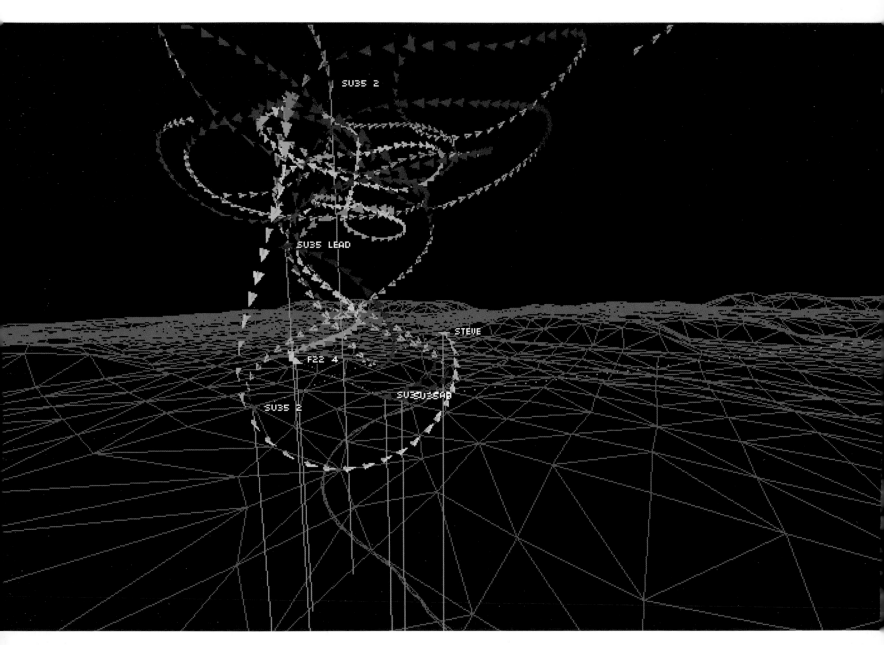

f-22 air dominance fighter I digital image design I ocean I pc I 1997

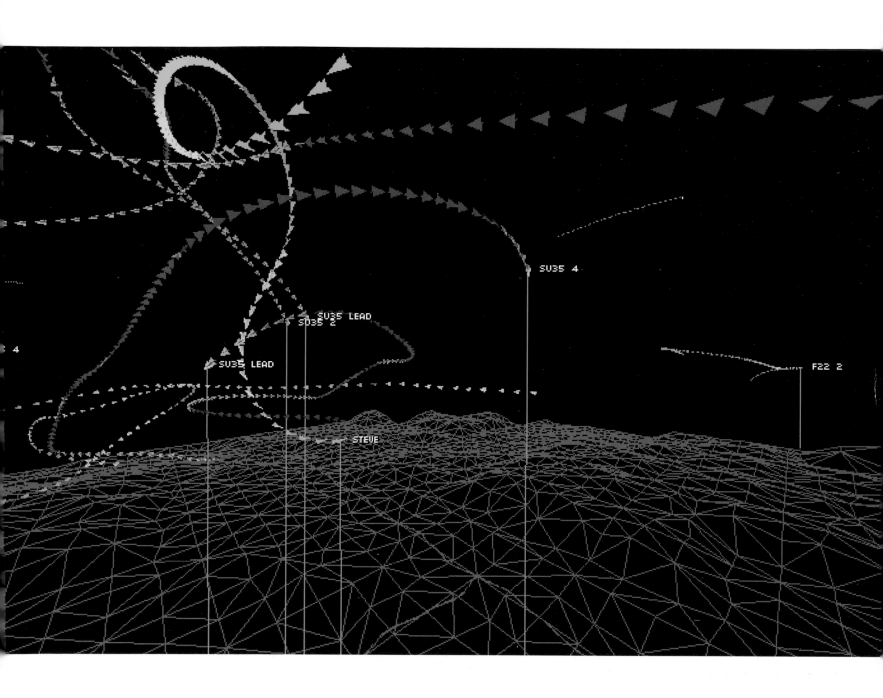

DATE DUE

index of games